Build Your Own
Kitchen Cabinets

DANNY PROULX

POPULAR WOODWORKING BOOKS
CINCINNATI, OHIO

SAFETY FIRST!

To prevent accidents, keep safety in mind while you work. Use the safety guards installed on power equipment; they are for your protection. When working on power equipment, keep fingers away from saw blades, wear safety goggles to prevent injuries from flying wood chips and sawdust, and wear headphones to protect your hearing.

DISCLAIMER

The author and editors who compiled this book have tried to make all the contents as accurate and as correct as possible. Plans, illustrations, photographs and text have been carefully checked. All instructions, plans and projects should be carefully read, studied and understood before beginning construction. Due to the variability of local conditions, construction materials, skill levels, etc., neither the authors, nor Popular Woodworking Books, assumes any responsibility for any accidents, injuries, damages or other losses incurred resulting from the material presented in this book.

02 01   6

Library of Congress Cataloging-in-Publication Data

Proulx, Danny.
    Build your own kitchen cabinets / by Danny Proulx.
        p. cm.
    Includes index.
    ISBN 1-55870-461-2 (pb : alk. paper)
    1. Kitchen cabinets. 2. Cabinetwork. I. Title
TT197.5.K57P76   1997
684.1'6—dc21   97-15260
                                                    CIP

Editor: R. Adam Blake
Content editor: Bruce E. Stoker
Production editor: Bob Beckstead
Interior designers: Brian Roeth and Jannelle Schoonover
Cover designer: Brian Roeth
Cover and interior color photography: Michael Bowie, Lux Photographic Services

METRIC CONVERSION CHART		
TO CONVERT	**TO**	**MULTIPLY BY**
Inches	Centimeters	2.54
Centimeters	Inches	0.4
Feet	Centimeters	30.5
Centimeters	Feet	0.03
Yards	Meters	0.9
Meters	Yards	1.1
Sq. Inches	Sq. Centimeters	6.45
Sq. Centimeters	Sq. Inches	0.16
Sq. Feet	Sq. Meters	0.09
Sq. Meters	Sq. Feet	10.8
Sq. Yards	Sq. Meters	0.8
Sq. Meters	Sq. Yards	1.2
Pounds	Kilograms	0.45
Kilograms	Pounds	2.2
Ounces	Grams	28.4
Grams	Ounces	0.04

DEDICATION

This book is dedicated to all my family and friends who have helped with this project—they've always been there to lend a hand—and to my wife, Gale, who has assisted me in the shop and provided the constructive criticism to make sure I produced the best product possible.

Most importantly, this book is a direct result of the support, guidance, and genuine concern of my editor at Betterway Books, Adam Blake. Without him, this project would not have been possible.

APPLYING THE TECHNIQUES

Start your project by reading Chapter One, "Designing and Building Your Own Kitchen Cabinets." Analyze your current kitchen, its good or bad points, and what added features or design changes are needed.

Understanding the anatomy of the cabinet designs in this system, their relationship to each other and function will lead you into the construction and assembly process.

To get the feel of the assembly procedures, begin by building a cabinet from an inexpensive sheet of any $5/8''$ material. Accurately cut the parts as detailed in the book, assemble the pieces and install the doors. It would be to your benefit to build both an upper and lower cabinet to get a feel of each style.

I believe, after you build your test cabinets, you'll see the value of this building system and the value in this building manual. Using the techniques in this book, you'll be able to build a beautiful set of kitchen cabinets. However, the best part is that you'll have saved many hundreds of dollars by building them yourself.

HOW TO USE THIS BOOK

Study this book with a systems approach in mind as you read. The cabinets are sized to accommodate the industry-standard doors and accessories. You'll soon be able to calculate the size of each cabinet component without referring to this book and quickly understand the relationship. As an example, a 36"-wide base cabinet has an inside dimension of 34"; therefore it requires two $17\frac{1}{2}''$-wide standard doors. It's as easy as it sounds.

This book is a step-by-step building manual rather than a general description of kitchen cabinetmaking. The dimensions, assembly procedures and techniques are tested and applied every day in my workshop.

TABLE OF CONTENTS

INTRODUCTION

Kitchen cabinetmaking, like many other skills, requires nothing more than attention to detail and patience. It's a skill that is learned and improved upon with practice and, I believe, well within the scope of most do-it-yourselfers.

The kitchen cabinetmaking style detailed in this book is a simple, straightforward style used by many cabinet manufacturers, with some minor variations. However, common dimensions such as cabinet depth, height and width, as well as the industry standard door sizes, govern the limits of those variations.

This building style was adapted from many sources. Primarily, it's a blend of the best features of European and North American style cabinetry. The carcass, or cabinet, is built with ⅝″ melamine-coated particle core board (PCB). A hardwood face frame is installed, taking the place of the European method of edge tape on the exposed PCB edges. Adjustable legs are installed on the base cabinets to maximize the cutting from a sheet of PCB and allow for easy cabinet installation. The hidden hinge is another European innovation used because of its strength, durability and ease of adjustment. The building system is logical and extremely adaptable to all situations, and the end result equals the best kitchen cabinets available.

Building kitchen cabinets requires basic woodworking skills along with some of the power and

The European or frameless style of cabinet on the left is a simple box made of melamine-coated particle core board with tape applied to cover the exposed PCB edges. The traditional or North American-style cabinet on the right is built with a wood face frame and often uses wood doors. The building style detailed in this book incorporates the positive aspects of the European cabinet with the beauty and strength of the traditional cabinet.

hand tools that most woodworkers own. Power tools include a table saw, circular saw, router and drills. Tools such as a radial arm saw, power screwdrivers and power sanders are always handy but not absolutely necessary. Obviously, the more "fancy" tools you have, and the more experienced you are with these tools, the quicker you will finish your projects. However, the end result is dependent on the attention to detail you put into the project and not primarily on the tools you own.

The most important piece of advice that I can

give anyone involves the planning and cutting of the cabinet parts. Take your time to plan the cutting process and accurately cut all the parts to the correct size. The assembly and finishing will be very simple if the cabinet pieces are accurately cut.

I have been involved in many areas of renovation work over the last twenty years, including home building, additions, basement finishing, kitchen and bathroom projects. The range has included building and installing a simple bathroom vanity to building a complete home. Over the last five years my specialty has been kitchen cabinets and kitchen renovation projects. Of all the building projects that I've completed, I consider kitchen cabinetmaking to be the most rewarding.

Today the focus of activity in the home is the kitchen or kitchen/family room area. We seem to be reverting back to earlier times when the kitchen was large and a meeting place for family and friends, as well as a place to prepare meals. Consequently, over the last five years, the emphasis seems to be toward larger kitchen and kitchen/family room combinations. New homes are being designed with larger kitchens and family or great rooms, as they are sometimes called, to meet those desires. Renovation projects involving the kitchen require that more space be allocated or, at the very least, that light colored or natural wood cabinets be used to make the room seem larger.

This trend toward larger kitchens has been beneficial to the kitchen cabinetmaking industry. Those of us who specialize in a "semi-custom" style cabinet have had even more of an increase in business because of all the special features people want installed in their new kitchen. Drawer pull-outs, lazy susans, pull-out pantry shelving and built-in cooktops and ovens are very popular and common features in the kitchens of today.

Most of the kitchens in the homes of the fifties and sixties were designed with a no-nonsense style and dark cabinets, simply as a place to quickly prepare a meal and leave. Now everyone wants to "hang out" in the kitchen. Remember the last time you had family and friends over for a meal: Where did everyone congregate? If it's anything like my place, all the guests were in the kitchen. We don't want a dark dungeon anymore. Most of us want a bright, airy, warm, comfortable room where we can prepare meals, chat with friends, make crafts or just relax in a cozy surrounding. From a personal point of view, I agree, there is nothing nicer than a large, bright, cozy kitchen. From a business point of view, I couldn't agree more; there are millions of older homes waiting for a kitchen renovation. And many of us are saving for the day when we can begin a kitchen renovation project.

To illustrate my point about the popularity of kitchen renovations, take a look in the yellow pages under Kitchen Cabinets and count the number of companies in your area. Also, look at most of the popular "how-to" shows on television and take note of the time given to kitchen projects. It's a very popular topic with most homeowners. Almost every time I meet someone new and they ask what I do for a living, their first comment is "That's interesting. You know, I really must do something about our kitchen. Maybe I'll give you a call." I don't always get a call, but it illustrates the interest in kitchen renovations.

Building kitchen cabinets is not difficult. All that is required is attention to detail and accurate cutting. Assembly of all the cut parts is simple when they are sized correctly. With a little time and effort, your final product will be beautiful.

With this book you can build yourself a beautiful quailty kitchen and stop there, or you can build for friends and family to recoup your costs. If you really enjoy the building process, you can open your own part-time or full-time kitchen cabinetmaking business. The choice is yours. There certainly is enough work to go around for the quality kitchen cabinetmaker.

CHAPTER ONE
Designing and Building Your Own Kitchen Cabinets

Fig. 1-1

Final adjustments on a standard base and upper cabinet

PLANNING YOUR KITCHEN

Nothing is more disruptive in a family's lifestyle than a major kitchen renovation project. Most family members spend a great deal of their time at home in the kitchen. This important room is used to prepare meals, for informal eating and as a casual gathering place for family and friends. People soon realize how important the room is when it's torn apart during renovations—even the simple task of making a cup of coffee becomes a major undertaking without a

kitchen. It is therefore critically important that tear-out and new installation are coordinated during the design phase to minimize down time. If you want a real-life definition of angry, tell someone that the kitchen will be down another week because you forgot to order something or your dimensions were wrong and you have to rebuild a cabinet.

Most experts agree that a kitchen renovation project will return almost 100 percent on investment when the property is sold. Surveys by the real estate industry show that a kitchen is one, if not the most, important feature with potential purchasers. Real estate agents have told me that the quality of the kitchen often makes or breaks the sale.

Kitchen design is very subjective. There are few hard-and-fast rules. A feature or layout that is perfect for one person is far from perfect for another. The issue of lifestyle and how it revolves around the kitchen is unique to each family. In most cases, the family, usually the prime user of the kitchen space, will have very definite ideas on what is needed and what the end result has to be to meet their needs. Often they have been looking through magazines, drawing rough floor plans, measuring and dreaming about their ideal kitchen for quite some time.

During the initial look at your existing

kitchen, research all of the information about new products and features on the market. Ask yourself questions about your requirements and put ideas on paper. Combine your notes and rough drawings along with accurate measurements and attempt to come up with two or three floor plans. I normally don't try to radically alter anything that will change a major feature that is important to me or my family; however, I will look at alternatives if I see something that is unsafe or very poorly designed. Try to incorporate the most important desires in alternative plans.

There are a few issues you should address during your initial look at the kitchen. Ask questions so that you understand all the needs. Consultants call it a needs analysis study, and although I don't go in for fancy titles, I think the term applies in this case.

Defining Your Needs

You will discover some interesting issues with this basic "self-test."

1. Discuss the existing kitchen space and layout with all the primary users of the kitchen in your household, listing the good and bad points of the design.
2. Investigate the traffic patterns in and through the kitchen.
3. Analyze the day-to-day meal preparation tasks. Try to formulate a "normal" daily meal preparation routine.
4. Ask your family questions about their desire to do more in the kitchen. Is there a hobby or area of interest, such as baking, that they would like to do more of if the added space or facilities were available?
5. Do you feel that a lot of walking or

movement is necessary during meal preparation?
6. Ask whether or not cleaning up after meals seems to be a monumental task. You may not solve that problem, but it may be reduced by simple layout changes.
7. You or your family might want to entertain more in the kitchen and only formally in the dining room if the kitchen space and functionality of the room could be improved.
8. Determine how long you plan to own the house. A $20,000 kitchen renovation project may not be fully recoverable if the intention is to upgrade for a quick sale in the near future. If you convince yourself to overimprove and the return is not realized during resale, you may possibly be wasting a good deal of money.
9. Discuss your family's wish list. If space or money was no object, what would you like to have in your dream kitchen?
10. Discuss topics such as lighting, both area and task illumination, kitchen seating needs and appliance upgrades.

There are other areas, which may surface during your investigation, that can be discussed. I've found being a good listener and asking many questions to be the best approach.

Kitchen design is a difficult process because everyone's needs and desires are different. I've designed and built cabinets and work spaces for kitchen renovation projects that I wouldn't have in my own personal kitchen, and I'm sure the reverse is true. Kitchen design is based on very personal and individual tastes.

Two design rules that seem to be true in every case deal with color and illumination. Light color or natural wood cabinets tend to brighten

Fig. 1-2

A typical U-shaped kitchen plan

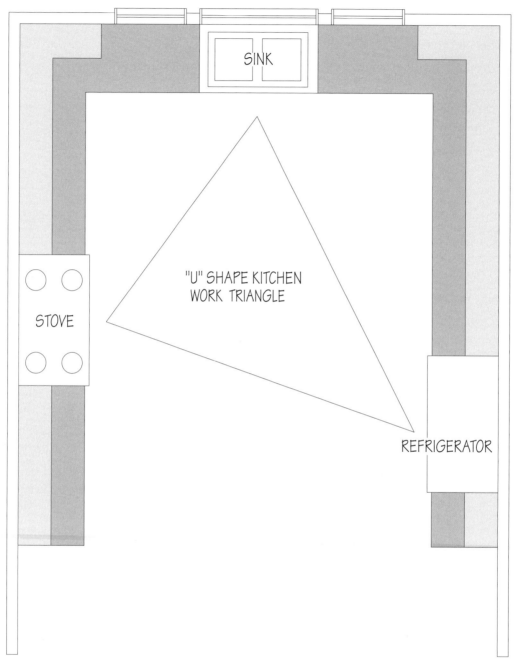

and visually enlarge a space, and improved general and task lighting always enhances the project. Older kitchens seemed to have dark cabinets and poor illumination, which gave you the impression you were in a cave. Yesterday's kitchen was simply a place to prepare the meal, clean up and leave the room. Today's lifestyle is very much focused on the kitchen as a gathering place for a wide and varied number of activities. The room has to be bright, seem large, be functional and adapt to many of those activities. Take your time and investigate all the alternatives as the planning stage is a very important process in any kitchen renovation project.

Fig. 1-3
A typical galley kitchen layout

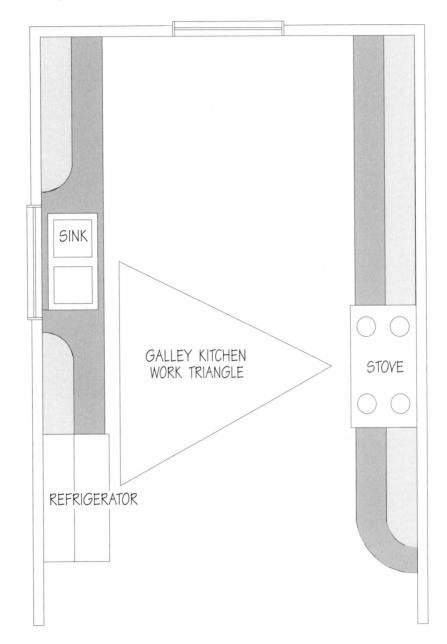

Choosing a Kitchen Style

There are many styles of kitchen layouts, including the L kitchen, galley, U-shaped and island styles, which can present many human traffic problems. In any style of kitchen, however, most kitchen designers agree that the sum of all the legs in a work triangle—the triangle formed by distances between the fridge to the stove to the sink and back to the fridge—be not less than 10′ and not greater than 25′. If the sum of the legs is too small, people will be tripping over each other and if it's too large, food preparation could be a very tiring task. I analyze this work pattern each time I design a kitchen layout, and

Fig. 1-4

The island kitchen is very popular when designing for a large room.

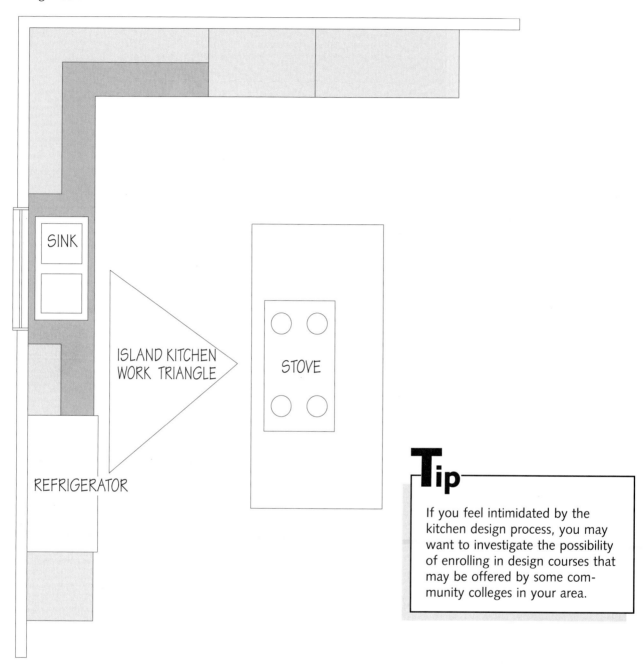

SINK

ISLAND KITCHEN
WORK TRIANGLE

STOVE

REFRIGERATOR

Tip

If you feel intimidated by the kitchen design process, you may want to investigate the possibility of enrolling in design courses that may be offered by some community colleges in your area.

it's proven to be a valuable exercise.

Kitchen design is a very important function, so much so that there are Certified Kitchen Designer certification programs. Individuals who are certified usually specialize in this area exclusively, which illustrates how vast the kitchen renovation field has become. There is a good living to be made with a great deal of satisfaction in the kitchen renovation field. However, like all specialized trades, knowledge comes from learning and the greatest teacher is experience. Read books, attend seminars and training programs and analyze every kitchen you come across for ideas and techniques.

KITCHEN DESIGN STANDARDS

There are certain accepted standards associated with kitchen cabinetmaking: counter height, space allowance between base and upper cabinets, cabinet depth and the space required for refrigerators and stoves. These dimensions are not cast in stone but are generally accepted in the industry, particularly by accessory and appliance manufacturers. The width of the majority of stoves is 30″, and normally a 31″ space is designed into the plan for stove installation. This gives us ½″ on each side of the stove so that it can be easily removed and replaced during cleaning or repair.

Refrigerators are not quite as standard as stoves, but a good rule of thumb is to allow 33″ for this appliance. The norm on most fridges is approximately 32″; however, check the existing appliance, or the one you plan to buy, before building.

The cabinet design detailed in this book is a modular blend of European and North American cabinet construction methods. The final product, once installed, looks more traditional because of the use of the face frame on the cabinet. The main difference between the two styles, traditional and European, is the use of the face frame. European cabinetry, in general terms, uses the same carcass style as is used in this design, after which the exposed carcass edges are covered with veneer tape or a laminate. In North American traditional-style cabinetry, the carcass edges are covered with a hardwood face frame. You'll also find detailed information on more traditional methods in this book.

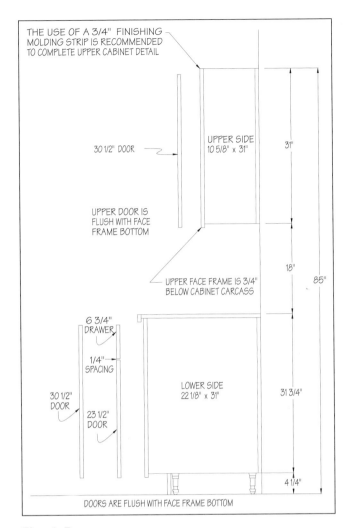

Fig. 1-5

There are common accepted standards for cabinet dimensions. Most appliance and accessory manufacturers use these dimensions when designing their products.

CABINET MATERIALS

The carcass of the standard cabinets, both uppers and bases, are built with ⅝" melamine particle core board (PCB). Both the upper and base cabinet back panels, unlike many cabinets on the market which are only ¼" or ½" thick, is a full ⅝"-thick PCB. This PCB back feature results in a cabinet that is of higher quality than most on the market today. Base and upper backing allows easier installation and a tighter cabinet, and eliminates the need to paint the walls inside and behind the cabinets. It also makes each cabinet a freestanding, strong, high-quality component.

Modifications or special cabinet carcass material can be substituted when the need arises. These include using ⅝" wood-veneer-covered PCB for microwave, pantry or glass door cabinets whose interiors will be exposed, as well as other special situations that will be discussed. In a kitchen I completed recently, the architect specified ¾" white melamine particle core board as

Fig. 1-6

The cabinet box (carcass) is the heart of this cabinet-building system.

the carcass material. This specification was easily met with only a minor width increase in the cabinet back board to accommodate the thicker carcass material. This cabinet design is so flexible that almost all special situations can be addressed with only very minor changes.

The face frame material for the standard cabinet is hardwood, normally oak, cherry, maple, birch and, in a few cases, walnut. The stiles (the vertical members of the face frame) are ¾" thick by 1" wide and 31¾" long. The rails (the horizontal pieces of the face frame) are ¾" thick by 1½" wide and 2" shorter than the overall width in the standard cabinet design. Another way of expressing rail width is that it is 1/16" shorter than the inside cabinet dimension. This applies to both the upper and base cabinet face frames.

Fig. 1-7

Various composite boards and hardwoods are used to build the cabinets. Shown are melamine particle core board, wood-veneer-covered particle core board, veneer plywood and hardwood for the face frames.

CABINET DOORS

Standard upper and base cabinets are full-height-door cabinets. Cabinet door height is variable, particularly on the base units, as the overall door height is dependent on whether or not a drawer assembly will be fitted above the door(s) in the cabinets. Special-size cabinets, such as those used over the stove, refrigerator and sink, need smaller doors to match the reduced cabinet height. However, these door sizes are stock items with most door manufacturers, as they are considered an industry standard.

Industry standard doors, used in this design on the uppers or base units without a drawer-over-door design, are 30½" high. Later in this book, under the drawer section, I will describe the door height requirements when installing drawers, flip-out assemblies or false drawer fronts in the base units. Reduced-height cabinets, such as those previously mentioned, will also be detailed under separate headings.

The standard cabinet sizes have a direct relationship to the door sizes produced by most manufacturers, both in height and width. Maintaining the basic cabinet sizes, where possible, allows us to use stock doors, which helps us build a high-quality cabinet in a reasonable price range.

The table on the next page illustrates the uniformity of the design, in that the same height door size is used on both the standard full door(s) upper and base cabinets.

Fig. 1-8

A cabinet door made from ¹¹/₁₆" veneer-covered particle core board with wood veneer edge tape

Fig. 1-9

Inexpensive and simple plywood doors can be used on cabinets for the workshop or laundry room.

Fig. 1-10

Medium-Density Fiberboard (MDF) doors are becoming a popular alternative.

Fig. 1-11

Solid-core hardwood cabinet doors are often the most expensive type of door.

STANDARD CABINET SIZES

Cabinet Size and Type	Door Width	Number of Doors
12″ Upper or Base	11½″	1
15″ Upper or Base	14½″	1
18″ Upper or Base	17½″	1
21″ Upper or Base	10″	2
24″ Upper or Base	11½″	2
27″ Upper or Base	13″	2
30″ Upper or Base	14½″	2
33″ Upper or Base	16″	2
36″ Upper or Base	17½″	2
24″ Upper Corner	14½″	1
36″ Corner Base	10″	2

Cabinet Doors—Building or Buying?

The issue of building your own or buying kitchen cabinet doors has been an ongoing point of debate for quite a long time. For years, prior to this kitchen cabinet design system, I made my own doors. Client desires were varied, and I spent a great deal of time and money investing in wood shapers and bits, as well as designing and building the necessary templates. When a large kitchen renovation project requires upwards of thirty doors, construction costs are a serious consideration and can affect the profit line. The door styles are numerous and, in the case of solid-core doors, labor for gluing up blanks, shaping and cutting adds up quickly. More often than not, the next client wanted a totally different door style, which again added to my cost. For this reason I now normally purchase factory-made doors. However, you may want to design and build your own doors, particularly if time is not an issue. I'll detail the process for building your own doors later in this book.

Today there are many, many door manufacturing companies that specialize in this area. A few are listed in the suppliers' section in the back of this book. As well, there is always the possibility of a sale or clearance on doors by a manufacturer or home store. That is another reason for designing your cabinets to accept industry-standard door sizes. During the research and design of this cabinet system, I quickly realized that as a cabinetmaking contractor I could not

Tip

Remember this important feature: These standard cabinet widths are specifically designed to accommodate the industry-standard cabinet door sizes. This feature allows you to purchase stock-production doors at a very reasonable cost.

hope to compete with the industry's pricing structure and offer the variety of styles that were available. Because they manufacture thousands of doors each month, their price is much lower and their selection is far greater than a small shop could hope to achieve.

The companies that supply doors are numerous, their lines are varied, the cost is very attractive and you can choose from an unlimited number of door styles. The added bonus is that these door companies are very competitive and want your business, no matter how small the order.

CABINET DESIGN

These cabinets have been designed without a center stile. Therefore, in the case where there are two doors on the cabinet, when the cabinet doors are open, you have complete access to the interior. This is made possible by the use of the fully adjustable European hinge. Each of the doors can be adjusted so that there is a $1/16''$ gap between them when closed. European hinges are installed on each door in a 35mm hole drilled on the inside of the door. They are high quality and simple to install, as I will detail in the upcoming sections of this book. The added advantage of European hinges is that they are hidden when the door(s) are closed so you don't have to worry about matching your hinge style to the door handle style. In about 90 percent of the applications I use the 120° full-overlay cabinet hinge.

The side boards, also called the cabinet gable ends, of the standard upper and base cabinets are the same length: 31″ long. Only the widths are different: $10\frac{5}{8}''$ wide for the uppers and $22\frac{1}{8}''$ wide for the base units. These dimensions allow for maximum use of a 4′ × 8′ standard sheet of melamine-coated particle core board for

carcass construction. The melamine sheets are 96″ long, which gives us three sides (3 × 31″ = 93″), and the side widths of the standard cabinet allow for four upper sides and two base sides across the 48″ width of the sheet. The interior depth of the standard uppers is $10\frac{5}{8}''$ plus the face frame thickness of $3/4''$ for a total interior depth of $11\frac{3}{8}''$ and the interior base depth is $22\frac{7}{8}''$.

Five pieces of melamine PCB are needed for the uppers: two side units, one top, one bottom and the back board. However, the base units require only four pieces: two sides, one bottom and one back. The top on the base is not required, as it is covered by the kitchen countertop assembly.

Base Cabinets
Base cabinets differ from uppers because they are fitted with European cabinet legs. These legs are independently adjustable, eliminate the need for a cabinet kick-plate base assembly, allow for a solid piece of 1″ × 4″ hardwood board to be

Fig. 1-12

Cabinet legs allow us to use a 31″ cabinet side for both the upper and lower cabinets. The cabinet side width is $10\frac{5}{8}''$ for uppers and $22\frac{1}{8}''$ for base units. These dimensions give maximum yield with very little waste when cutting the 4′ × 8′ sheet material.

clipped on as the toe kick, and make installation very easy and accurate. These legs permit us to use 31″ cabinet gables, which maximize the yield from a standard sheet of 4′ × 8′ PCB board. Once you use this European cabinet leg system, you'll never want to return to the traditional methods of longer sides and 2″ × 4″ cabinet base support frames that are difficult to level and shim during cabinet installation.

The issue of maximum function and use of the interior of the cabinet was also of major concern during my research into a cabinetry system. The majority of systems in the marketplace have opted for adjustable shelving as a standard design feature in all the cabinets, particularly the upper cabinets. The base units tend to feature adjustable shelving and pull-outs on European drawer slides. The base corner cabinet usually has the 32″ pie-cut lazy susan system installed. These design decisions offered the most flexibility, were very functional and, from a construction standpoint, were easy to incorporate into the design.

Fig. 1-14

The completed upper cabinet is very traditional in appearance.

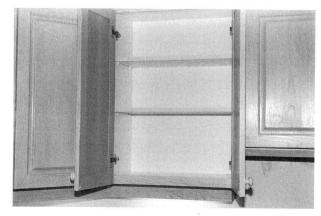

Fig. 1-15

Complete access to the upper cabinet space is possible because we don't use a center stile.

Upper Cabinets

The upper cabinets are a very important and integral part of this design system. Quite a lot of design consideration has been given to these cabinets, as they are the most widely used and most often accessed. Plates, glasses, spices and food products are stored in these units. And if you stop and think about how many times a day they are used, you'll realize how important they are to the overall design.

Upper cabinets are designed for easy access as well as allowing for a degree of customization

Fig. 1-13

36″ corner base cabinet with 32″ pie-cut lazy susan installed

by the homeowner so that they can be adapted to their particular needs. These cabinets must also be easy to clean, as they will be subject to a great deal of abuse. The main features are the melamine-coated interior and the adjustable shelving.

Shelving

The cabinets in this system use the adjustable shelf as a standard. It provides you with an efficient and flexible cabinet which is very well accepted. Normally, I will install two adjustable shelves in each standard upper cabinet with a 2″ position adjustment. The upper corner cabinet is almost exclusively fitted with an 18″ full-round, two-shelf lazy susan.

Base cabinets are constructed with one adjustable shelf, or one, and possibly two, pull-out drawer assemblies depending on client needs. The corner base is almost always fitted with a 32″ pie-cut, two-shelf lazy susan assembly.

Shelving is made out of the same ⅝″ melamine-coated particle core board. The front or exposed edge of the PCB can be covered with a plastic edging called cap molding. You can also face the shelf with hardwood. I normally construct full-depth base shelves to maximize the storage space of the cabinet.

Fig. 1-16
The adjustable shelf pins allow you to customize the interior space to fit your needs.

Fig. 1-17
An upper corner cabinet equipped with an 18″ round lazy susan

Fig. 1-18
⅝″ plastic cap molding installed on shelf-front edge

Tip

If the shelving is longer than 30″ wide, I often install a 1″×2″ hardwood cleat, running the full width of the shelf on the rear underside of the shelf board, for added rigidity. Shelves tend to be loaded quite heavily, and I want the longer shelves strong so they won't sag or break under heavy loads.

PARTICLE CORE BOARD HARDWARE

The basis of this cabinet design is the construction of a very strong carcass or box as the body for each modular cabinet. The ⅝″ particle core board is butt joined and secured with 2″ PCB screws every four inches. These screws are called particle board or chip board screws and are available at most large home centers and through the sources in the appendix. The wood face frame is constructed using butt joints, glue and two wood screws at each joint. Other joining options include biscuits, pocket screws on the rear of the face frame or a mortise-and-tenon joint. This wood face frame is then attached to the carcass front using glue and 2″ spiral finishing nails. Nails are countersunk and the holes are covered with colored wood filler wax, making them almost invisible. If you want to avoid nailing and filling, you can use biscuits.

However, under normal circumstances, the cabinet door, when closed, covers the filled nail holes.

PARTICLE CORE BOARD MATERIAL

One very important issue that you have to address is the quality of the melamine-coated particle core board. It's the heart of the system and must be of the highest quality. Don't be tempted to use bargain-priced PCB; it will only lead to serious problems. High-quality screw-fastened butt joints are dependent on high-grade PCB. There are many grades of PCB on the market, and many are not suitable for good-quality carcass construction. I use an industrial grade, sometimes called a cabinet grade by some manufacturers, PCB with a rated strength of 43 pounds per cubic foot. Manufacturers' ratings may differ,

Fig. 1-19

The particle board screw

Fig. 1-20

⅝″ melamine PCB butt joined with 2″ particle core board screws

Fig. 1-21

The face frame can be butt joined using the same PCB screws.

however. Investigate the supply in your area and buy the highest grade available; it is cheaper in the long run. One visual clue that might be useful is the density, size and compacting of the wood chip in the PCB. The denser and finer the chips in the boards are, and ones that appear to be tightly compacted, usually indicate a high-quality board. However, take some time to compare the specifications of the different PCB material available in your area. Study the material, ask questions and become well informed on PCB material; it will pay high dividends.

Tip

Melamine-coated PCB is rated by the paper density covering the board. The board you purchase should have a minimum surface paper rating of 135 grams. The core of the board should carry an industrial-grade rating.

DRAWERS

Drawers are an important and integral component in any kitchen renovation project. The majority of kitchens have a four-drawer bank for cutlery and utensils, plus additional drawers in base cabinets. Microwave cabinets with a lower drawer bank are also an extremely popular addition to the modern kitchen.

In keeping with the design of the cabinets, I wanted to construct drawers that were sturdy, reasonably priced and easy to maintain. Since the drawer would be opened and closed many thousands of times throughout the life of the kitchen, I wanted a strong, well-constructed carcass. The cost of manufacturing the drawer, as well as the retail price to the client, was also a very important issue. Solid wood drawers would be strong but expensive, so a construction method based on melamine-coated particle core board seemed to be the answer. If constructed properly, they would be very sturdy. The cost would be reasonable because PCB strips for the sides, fronts and backs were left over after cutting the cabinet carcass pieces from the $4' \times 8'$ sheets of material. Also, the melamine surface would be easy to maintain when the drawers needed cleaning.

There are many drawer designs on the market, including solid wood, combinations of melamine PCB and metal, and all-melamine PCB material. I decided, based on my research, to construct a drawer carcass in much the same fashion as the cabinet carcass. Using industrial-grade 5/8" melamine-coated PCB for the sides, back, front and bottom, fastened with 2" PCB screws in combination with high-quality European drawer slides, in a box fashion as indicated, produced an excellent product. A wood face is attached to the box acting as the drawer face and is either purchased from your cabinet

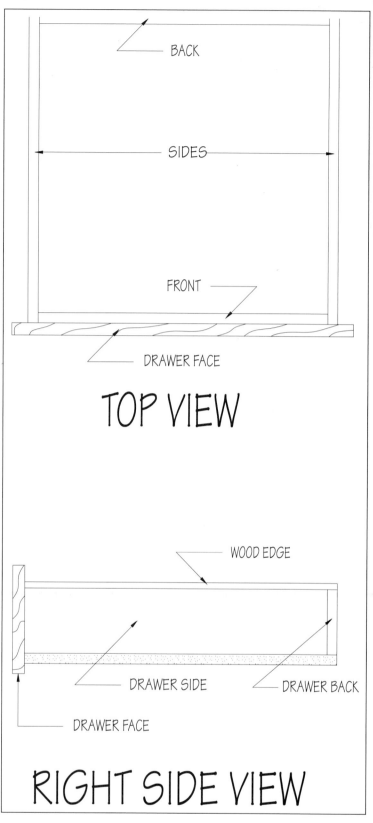

Fig. 1-22

The drawer box is constructed of 5/8" melamine with wood edges and a hardwood face.

door supplier or made from solid 1″ × 8″ material as I often do. The solid wood drawer face can be cove or round-over edge routered to match the style of the cabinet doors you are installing.

I have been using this method of construction for about three years, and I have not had any major drawer problems. The drawer carcass is heavy due to the weight of the PCB material, making it operate very smoothly. The melamine coating makes cleaning very easy, and you do not have to line the drawers with protective paper. This drawer style has been very well received by my clients not only because it looks good and is easy to maintain, but also because of the low cost of the unit. The exposed top edge of the melamine PCB for the drawer box can be covered with melamine iron-on veneer tape or with ⅝″-wide strips of ¼″-thick solid wood strips that are rounded over and finished. The wood edge on the drawers is the same wood as the cabinets and is an extremely attractive accent detail when the drawer is opened.

Drawer construction material is not limited to melamine PCB. You can use just about any material available. Plywoods such as Baltic Birch, which is sometimes called cabinet-grade plywood and is void free, can be used, as well as any of the solid hardwoods to match the wood you've chosen to build your kitchen.

Solid wood drawers can be joined by using the common butt joint or the more involved finger or dovetail joints. The choice is yours.

Pull-Outs

Base cabinet pull-outs can be a ⅝″ melamine PCB box, much like the drawer carcass—particularly when a deep pull-out is required for pots and pans storage—with a solid wood face. Another option that I often use is a piece of ⅝″

Fig. 1-23
½″ cabinet-grade plywood, sometimes called Baltic Birch, can also be used for drawer boxes.

Fig. 1-24
Solid-wood drawer boxes with dovetail joints are another option.

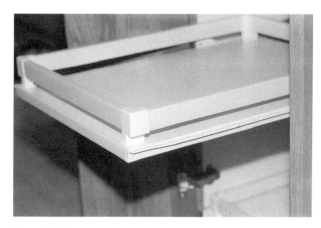

Fig. 1-25

Pull-out shelf with PVC drawer surround

Fig. 1-26

Pull-out shelves can also be made of hardwood with ¼" plywood bottoms.

Fig. 1-27

A deep pull-out, much like the standard PCB drawer box, can also be constructed.

melamine PCB with veneer edges to cover the exposed PCB, in combination with European drawer slides. A rail system, as shown in the photo at left, called a PVC drawer surround, is another excellent alternative for base cabinet pull-outs.

You can design and build any style of pull-out using a variety of materials. The options are limitless as this is an area that can be personally customized to meet your requirements. A few options I've used include solid wood pull-outs with rails, melamine PCB with hardwood rails and extra-deep pull-outs for garbage and recycling bins.

Tip

The pull-out you design must fit on the bottom-mounted drawer glides—with the exception of this rule, anything you imagine can be constructed.

BATHROOM CABINETS

Bathroom renovations are as popular as kitchen renovations. Wood cabinets in light natural finishes seem to be the most popular application. Bathrooms, like kitchens, are being given more space during the design process in new construction and renovation projects in existing homes. The trend seems to be toward larger, brighter and more functional bathrooms with whirlpools, shower stalls and all the other new fixtures that are available.

In the past, the homeowner could go out to the local building center and purchase a standard-size vanity cabinet for their bathroom renovation project. One cabinet for the sink and the project was finished. Today the demand is for cabinets of varying width, height and function. Drawer banks, corner cabinets and pantry units in the bathroom are becoming very common.

All the standard cutting and assembly principles can be applied when building specialized bathroom cabinets. The only major difference is the finished cabinet height. There doesn't seem to be a standard height for bathroom cabinets. I've seen cabinets as low as 28″ and as high as the standard kitchen base cabinet at 36″. In the last few years a cabinet height of 34″ appears to be the most popular.

Cabinet height requirements for bathroom cabinets can be easily achieved by simply changing the height of the sides and back. For example, if you require a run of 34″-high cabinets, reduce the dimension by 2″. The base sides and back would be 29″ high instead of the normal 31″. All other standards, as previously discussed, would be used to build the units.

Upper cabinet size and assembly procedures for the bathroom are identical to the standard applications, with the exception of cabinet depth. Bathroom upper cabinets are not as deep as the standard kitchen upper cabinets. However, an alteration in depth is easily accomplished by reducing the width of the sides, bottom and top boards. Cabinets over the sink base may be only 6″ deep, which means the boards would be ripped at 4⅝″ instead of the normal 10⅝″. All the other standard assembly procedures would be applicable.

Cabinet end finishing, adjustable shelving using the hole jig and door fitting are identical to the standard cabinet assembly procedures. The adjustable leg feature of this cabinet system is a real benefit in a bathroom application because water on the bathroom floor is a common occurrence. Heating, plumbing and electrical installation needs, often a real problem in the confined bathroom space, are more effectively met because of the added space under the cabinets provided by the cabinet legs and removable toe kick board.

Fig. 1-28

A modified-height base cabinet was built for this basement bathroom. The toe kick board was not installed because of the danger of water on the floor. Because this cabinet has plastic adjustable legs, the possibility of water damage has been eliminated.

Fig. 1-29

An upper cabinet was built using this system and installed over the toilet for added storage. Notice that we've reduced the depth of the cabinet sides from 10⅝″ to 4″ to fit the requirements.

CHAPTER TWO
Tools

I've noticed that many "how-to" books include a section on tools, and I feel there is some merit in discussing this issue. Good tools are your most important asset. However, I don't want to dedicate twenty pages to screwdrivers and hand saws, as I believe most readers of this book are beyond that point. This chapter is a general discussion of tools and a few tricks that I've learned over the years. I hope some of the tips might make your project progress smoother.

BITS AND BLADES

Generally, it's important that your cutting equipment is carbide tipped. Saw blades, countersink and router bits will last much longer than high-speed steel when cutting the high-glue-content particle core boards. Though initially more expensive, carbide-tipped tools will cost less in the long run.

Edge chips on melamine-coated particle core board are a fact of life when cutting this material. However, damage can be minimized by using a triple-chip saw blade. You'll also notice that the saw "chips" the board on one side and is relatively chip free on the other. Orient the boards during the cutting process so the good side is always in the same direction relative to the saw table. Make sure the blade is sharp and in good shape and the depth of cut is set only slightly greater than the thickness of the board.

Fig. 2-1
A "triple-chip" or "veneer" blade is specifically designed for cutting melamine PCB. If kept sharp, it will minimize the amount of tear-out when cutting.

Fig. 2-2
A well-tuned table saw will make cutting 4' × 8' sheets a simple task.

TABLE SAW

The table saw is my most important asset; it is also the most dangerous. I've visited the hospital emergency ward on one occasion because I wasn't paying proper attention during the sawing operation. Be very careful, read the safety rules for your equipment and don't work when you're tired. Accidents can happen faster than you can imagine.

You'll hear and read many discussions regarding the value of a table saw vs. a radial arm saw. If your budget allows you to purchase only one of the two, which one should you buy? I don't want to add to the confusion; however, I would definitely purchase the table saw. It's an extremely versatile piece of equipment. And if you do decide to purchase a table saw, buy the most powerful one you can afford. A good-quality 3-horsepower saw will give you many years of excellent service.

Tips

- To achieve maximum cutting quality, make sure your table saw fence is perfectly parallel to the saw blade and your blades are as sharp as possible. Measure the distances from the front of the blade and the back of the blade to the fence. They should be the same.
- Verify the fence-to-saw blade distance each time you change blades, as not all saw blades are the same thickness.
- To make cutting the 4′ × 8′ sheets easier, reduce the drag on the material by applying a good-quality paste wax or paraffin to the table of the saw and the surface of your feed tables. You'll be amazed how much easier it is to cut the sheet goods when the friction is minimized.
- Purchase high-quality carbide blades and drill bits. They're more expensive than high-speed steel, but they'll last longer, give better results and in the long run you'll save money and frustration.

Cutting 4′ × 8′ sheets of particle core board or plywood with anything other than a table saw is a difficult job. Nothing can match the accuracy and consistency of the tool. It's possible to use a radial arm saw for cutting sheet goods, but the process is much more difficult. Two cuts, halfway through the board, are necessary when cutting the wider base cabinet boards on a radial arm saw. With an accessory called a panel cutter, which can be purchased or homemade for your table saw, cutting wide pieces to size after the sheets are ripped is an easy job.

With this cabinet building system, only the shelf boards and drawer sides show both surfaces of the material. To virtually eliminate edge chipping with these pieces, set the saw blade to just over half the thickness of the board for the first cut and then flip the board over and finish the cut. This process isn't absolutely perfect, but you'll have to look very close to see any edge damage.

The ideal accessory for cutting melamine-coated particle core board on a table saw is a scoring blade. A small secondary blade scores the underside of the PCB before it enters the main blade. However, this is a very expensive option and would only be worthwhile if you plan to cut quite a number of boards. Remember, with this cabinet building system, we only have to deal with a couple of pieces that show both sides.

At one time I could purchase 4′ × 8′ sheets of melamine-coated PCB with finished cuts on four edges of the board. Now, due to production costs and other issues that I'm not privy to, the supplier sells these boards without these nice finished cabinet-ready edges. Prior to cutting to size, I must cut the board so I have a good edge. The manufacturer in your area may supply dressed four-edge PCB; if not, you'll have to dress an edge on the saw. The simplest method is with a table saw that has a fence system capable of ripping a 49″-wide board. If your saw isn't equipped with an extended fence system, you can dress the edge with a circular saw and then cut the sheet on a table saw. Another method that I often use is to cut the sheet into slightly oversized pieces with a circular saw and then trim these easier-to-handle smaller sections of the sheet to the exact size. Square, straight cuts will make the cabinet assembly process much simpler. Verify that your saw fence is parallel to the blade and that the distance gauge is accurate.

Support Rollers and Tables

Infeed and outfeed rollers on your table saw improve the cuts and reduce fatigue. Tables can be made very simply or you can purchase roller assemblies. Cutting a 4′ × 8′ sheet is awkward, so I'd recommend you have someone help you with this phase of the building process. With a second set of hands and the feed rollers, the results will be much improved and you won't be as tired.

Fig. 2-3
A table saw accessory called a slide table is a nice option when cutting ripped panels to size.

Fig. 2-4
An outfeed roller aids in the sheet-cutting process.

Fig. 2-5

There are many routers available and an unlimited choice of router bits.

ROUTERS

The router is another important tool in your workshop. The newest style heavy-duty plunge router is ideal and versatile. It's well worth considering if you are planning on purchasing one router for all your work. With the money saved building your own kitchen cabinets, you may consider purchasing two routers, one heavy-duty model for back board trimming and countertop round-over edge work, and a smaller laminate trim router. You can very easily operate with one router, but if your budget can handle the added expense, the second is a nice addition. The heavy-duty model, equipped with a good carbide-edge trim bit, will easily cut 5/8" PCB. The same router equipped with a round-over bit can be used when you assemble and finish the custom countertop described in this book.

Small laminate trim routers are easy to handle and work extremely well when you have to flush trim high-pressure laminate material. However, any size router will accomplish this task.

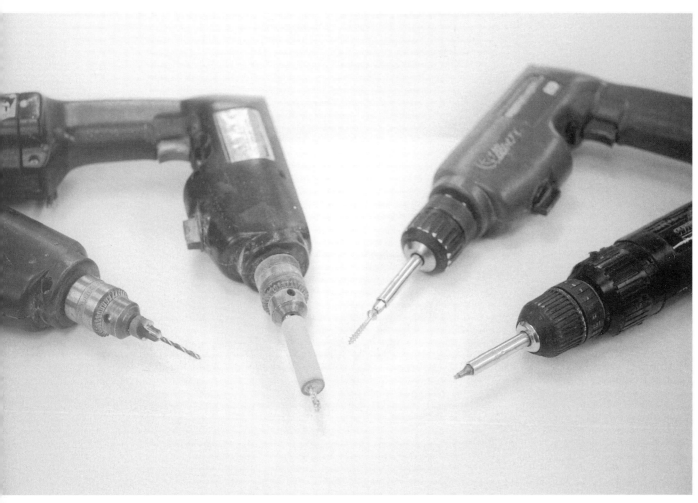

Fig. 2-6
Cordless drills as well as the standard corded models are useful items. Drills can be fitted with ⅜″ countersink drill bits, regular bits and screwdriver attachments.

CORDLESS DRILL/DRIVER

The heavy-duty cordless screwdriver makes screw insertion go much faster. It is invaluable in a kitchen project that normally requires between five hundred and one thousand screws. I can remember using a hand screwdriver for the majority of my fastening, so I know firsthand how it simplifies work. Buy the best quality you can afford in a 12V model, if possible.

A good drill equipped with a ⅛″ bit and ⅜″ countersink assembly that is carbide tipped is necessary. A cordless drill is nice but not mandatory, particularly when the corded drill is relatively inexpensive. It's important that you drill a pilot hole for every screw used to join particle core board and the hardwood face frames. Without this pilot hole, the joint will fail.

POWER SANDERS

Power sanders in the random orbital and palm styles are another good investment. I rough sand with 100- and 150-grit paper on the random orbital sander and finish with 180-grit paper by hand and with the palm sander. Both sanders have an orbital action so you can sand with or against the grain.

DRILL PRESS

The 35mm flat bottom hole in the door, used for hinge mounting, is best made with a drill press. The unit doesn't have to be large or fancy. It simply has to hold the drill bit at a right angle to the door. I have drilled this hinge hole by hand, but the results are not as accurate. Most small drill presses are reasonably priced and can be used for many other projects.

Fig. 2-7

There are many sanders available at reasonable prices. One recent innovation that was adapted from the auto body repair industry is the random orbital sander, which has made wood sanding a lot easier.

Fig. 2-8

In my shop I use a multipurpose tool that can be adapted for use as a drill press. However, there are small benchtop models that are inexpensive and more than capable of drilling holes for the door hinges. A carbide-tipped 35mm drill bit is used for these holes.

GALLERY OF KITCHENS

Years ago, kitchen cabinets were built without too much thought about interior use and function. Shelves were fixed in place and finished with a coat of paint. Most cabinets required the homeowner to paint the kitchen walls that could be seen inside the cabinets and cover the cabinet shelves with paper. Today, modern kitchens have many appliances, work-saving devices and accessories that are considered a must. Dishwashers, wall ovens and cooktops; pasta makers, bread makers, automatic coffee makers, all require space in the kitchen. Standard features with today's kitchen cabinets include adjustable shelves, maintenance-free interiors, lazy susans, functional corner cabinets, drawer banks and base and pantry cabinet pull-outs, and cabinets can be customized for specific tasks or hobbies. All these features make today's kitchen an exciting place to work and gather with friends.

The following pages showcase seven different kitchens I've worked on. Note that each employs all of the basic skills explained in the book, but also note that each one is unique. All have been built in kitchens of different sizes for families with different needs, but each one comes from the same basic mold. Whether you are doing new construction or remodeling, you can make any of these kitchens work for you.

I've given you sort of a wishbook for your own kitchen. Take a look at your own kitchen and envision it remodeled in the same fashion as one of the featured kitchens. You may want to keep the same basic look your old cabinets had; so copy your old door styles and modify them for use with new cabinets. You may want to keep the same look but have your cabinets serve different purposes; so rebuild the same configuration of upper and lower cabinets, but add a lazy susan here or a flip-out there. Or instead of drawers, install cabinets with pull-out shelves.

Maybe you need to increase your storage space; grab some space-saving ideas from the end of the gallery where I've given you some examples of pull-outs, flip-outs and lazy susans.

Or you may want to go for an entirely different look. Add an island or a peninsula. Enclose your microwave oven or refrigerator. Change the color of your kitchen with different woods, finishes and countertop surfaces.

U-SHAPED KITCHENS

The U-shaped kitchen is pretty much a medium size layout, though it easily suits a smaller kitchen, as in an apartment or small home. Obviously, as the name implies, the layout is against three walls, and the work triangle, as indicated by the drawing on page 10, usually falls in the center of the room.

This kitchen features solid wood doors that are carved with a wheat design. The custom countertop is featured on page 100. Take note of the refrigerator surround and pantry combination unit.

L-SHAPED KITCHENS

This is an example of a kitchen design in an apartment with limited space. Unfortunately, the client had not yet completed the tile backsplash. The kitchen features a built-in upper cabinet microwave and toaster oven shelf. There is a refrigerator surround and pantry to maximize storage space. To take advantage of all the space available, the upper cabinets were extended to the ceiling. We also installed an oak surround florescent lighting fixture to provide even illumination to the work area.

GALLEY KITCHENS

The galley kitchen is reminiscent of shipboard kitchens, or galleys: long and narrow, much like the typical small apartment layout. Your work triangle is not all that big and, depending on how the plumbing, gas and electric lines were run, it may be in a straight line down one side of the room, as it is in this example. Fortunately, this kitchen takes advantage of built-in microwave oven and wall oven cabinets to save much needed floorspace. The cabinets are finished with a whitewash stain and two coats of polyurethane.

GALLEY KITCHENS

This kitchen is an example of the walk-through galley design. You've got both walls to utilize, and a little more space for your work triangle. Take note of the unique microwave space above a small drawer in the upper cabinet. Also notice how the window fits into the design with a curved valance that provides an unbroken visual line.

These countertops are also the custom style described on page 100. The cabinets are finished with three coats of clear polyurethane.

ISLAND KITCHEN

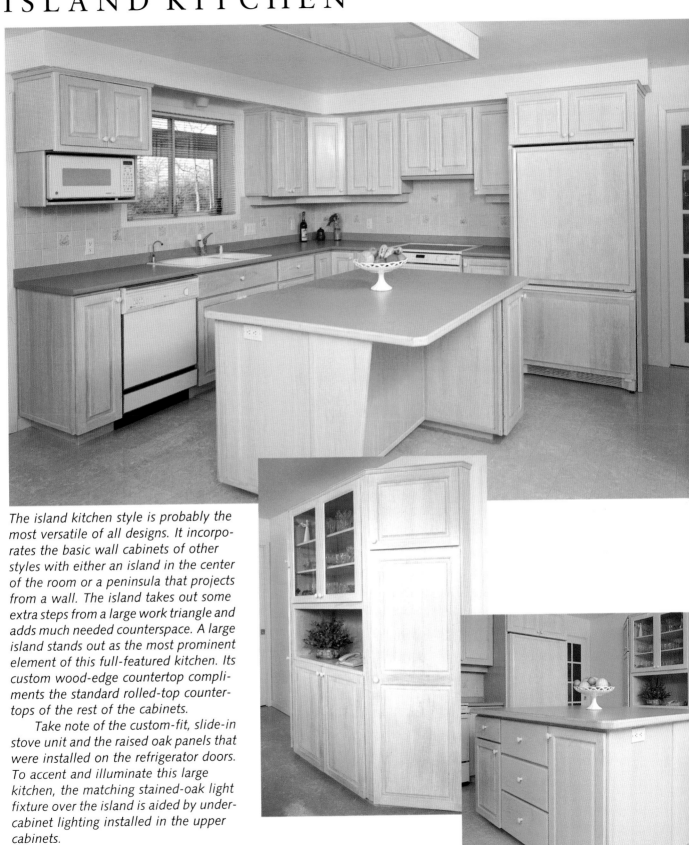

The island kitchen style is probably the most versatile of all designs. It incorporates the basic wall cabinets of other styles with either an island in the center of the room or a peninsula that projects from a wall. The island takes out some extra steps from a large work triangle and adds much needed counterspace. A large island stands out as the most prominent element of this full-featured kitchen. Its custom wood-edge countertop compliments the standard rolled-top countertops of the rest of the cabinets.

Take note of the custom-fit, slide-in stove unit and the raised oak panels that were installed on the refrigerator doors. To accent and illuminate this large kitchen, the matching stained-oak light fixture over the island is aided by under-cabinet lighting installed in the upper cabinets.

ISLAND KITCHEN

The island added to this kitchen is really a peninsula. It offers that bonus of extra counterspace without taking up premium floorspace in a medium-size kitchen. In this case, the peninsula adds some needed cabinet space and a breakfast bar, and it also sets the kitchen apart from the eating area a little more.

A unique feature of this kitchen is the combination refrigerator surround and pantry unit the depth of the refrigerator. The oak hardwood floor and high crown moulding give the whole kitchen a traditional, country-style look.

ISLAND KITCHEN

This kitchen—mine—has a peninsula that extends the wall with 12' of additional cabinet, and counterspace that doubles as a sit-down breakfast bar. The main feature is the use of $^{11}/_{16}''$ veneer-covered PCB for the doors, a low-cost alternative to solid wood doors. The kitchen also features a built-in oven, microwave pantry, cooktop stove and a refrigerator surround. The pantry and base cabinets have pull-out shelves. The upper cabinets have under-cabinet lighting.

CABINET ACCESSORIES

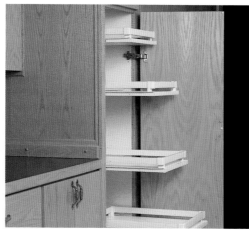

Pull-out shelves are a combination of shelves and drawers. Instead of searching through a stack of pots and pans in your lower cabinets, just slide out the shelf and pick what you need. Build your own using drawer slides.

Perhaps the simplest innovation for customizing your cabinets and maximizing storage space is adjustable shelving. You can change shelf heights to accommodate what you are storing, and when you want to rearrange the kitchen, it is as simple as moving a few shelf pins.

Utilize wasted corner space by installing a lazy susan. In upper cabinets, use a regular corner cabinet with 170° full-overlay hinges.

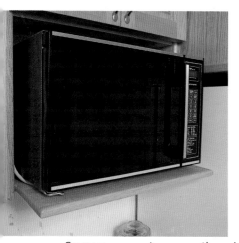

Many times kitchen cabinet-makers put a false drawer front in front of the sink so that it matches the rest of the drawers and cabinets. Why not use the four or five inches of dead space under the cabinet for a flip-out to store dish soap, sponges and other small items?

Save your counterspace, though perhaps at the expense of some cabinet space, by putting your microwave or toaster oven on a shelf.

CHAPTER THREE
Kitchen Cabinet Anatomy

There are specific names identifying cabinet parts used throughout the book. These names simply describe the various parts of a cabinet and are widely used in the industry.

An upper cabinet carcass is made up of five pieces: two sides, a back, top and bottom. The standard base is constructed with two sides, a back and a bottom. The base units have adjustable legs and don't require a top because the countertop sits on the cabinet. See Figure 3-2 for standard cabinet assembly.

HYBRID CABINET PARTS

A hardwood face frame is constructed and installed to replace the European method of taping the PCB edges on a frameless-style cabinet. This face frame gives the cabinet a North American appearance. Face frame components consist of vertical members called stiles and horizontal members called rails.

You may notice that this building system eliminates the center stile, which was traditional on older North American cabinets. There are many important reasons why this stile is left out on these hybrid cabinets. With a center stile in place, you wouldn't be able to install pull-out drawers in the base cabinets. Access to the cabinet interior is improved by eliminating this member, and installing adjustable shelves is much easier. We can now build the cabinet without the

Fig. 3-1

Hybrid cabinets, such as the upper (right) and lower cabinets shown here, utilize European-style carcass construction and hinges with traditional North American face frames, combining the benefits of easy, modern construction with modern materials and traditional appearance.

center stile because of the high-quality European hidden hinge. It is stronger, more durable and can be adjusted sideways, in a vertical plane, or toward or away from the cabinet face frame. The hinge will allow you to adjust the gap between doors on a two-door cabinet to very close tolerances, and it will hold the position.

European Hinge

The high quality of this cabinet-building system depends in part on the European door hinge and

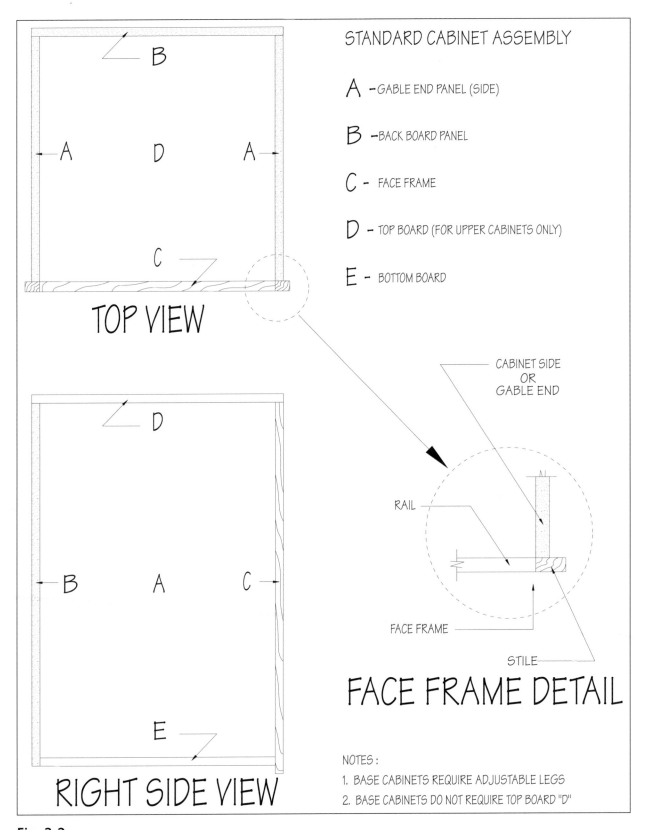

STANDARD CABINET ASSEMBLY

A — GABLE END PANEL (SIDE)

B — BACK BOARD PANEL

C — FACE FRAME

D — TOP BOARD (FOR UPPER CABINETS ONLY)

E — BOTTOM BOARD

TOP VIEW

RIGHT SIDE VIEW

CABINET SIDE
OR
GABLE END

RAIL

FACE FRAME

STILE

FACE FRAME DETAIL

NOTES :
1. BASE CABINETS REQUIRE ADJUSTABLE LEGS
2. BASE CABINETS DO NOT REQUIRE TOP BOARD "D"

Fig. 3-2

This illustration details the upper cabinet parts. The names for the base cabinet are identical. Base cabinets do not require a top board and differ from uppers because they have adjustable cabinet legs installed.

Fig. 3-3

The European hidden hinge can be adjusted in three directions.

Since the hinges are hidden, style is not a major consideration. In effect, we don't have to be concerned that the hinges will match the choice of handles.

With our construction method we use a 1″ stile covering the side edge as our standard. We also use a full-overlay Euro hinge as the standard hinge; therefore, the door will overlap ⅝″ of the stile, leaving ⅜″ exposed. The result is a traditional-looking cabinet style.

Hinges are classified by degrees of opening. A 90° hinge will allow the door to swing fully open at a right angle to the face frame. For the

its ability to adjust in three directions. The design of this hinge allows for very accurate placement of the cabinet doors because of the hinge's mechanical ability to hold that placement. Because the European hinge was developed for and is almost exclusively used on European-style cabinetry or cabinets without the traditional North American face frame, hinge styles are named in reference to the European cabinet. A full-overlay European hinge is meant to fully cover or overlay the side edge of the cabinet. Carcass thickness is normally ⅝″, so a full-overlay European hinge covers approximately ⅝″ of the cabinet face. I say approximately because metric measure is widely used with these hinges, as they are European based, and there is a slight difference. However, for our purposes we can assume a full-overlay hinge covers ⅝″ of the cabinet face and a half-overlay hinge covers approximately 5/16″ of the face.

The high quality of this hinge is the reason why it's incorporated in this cabinet design. The other reason is one of cost. Although initially it can be more expensive than the traditional hinges, you only require two or three types.

Fig. 3-4

This is one of the many styles of adjustable cabinet legs that are available. The screw holds the leg to the cabinet base board and the colored cover cap hides the screw head.

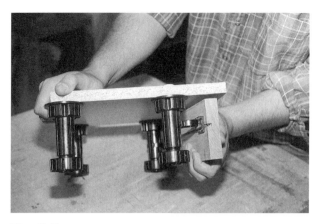

Fig. 3-5
The toe kick board simply clips onto the leg with an assembly called a plinth clip.

Fig. 3-6
Two of the four runners of the drawer glide assembly are mounted on the cabinet side, and the remaining two are screwed to the drawer bottom.

majority of situations I use a 120° hinge. As you will see, applications such as the corner base cabinet, with a lazy susan installed, require a wider degree of door opening to provide easy access to the cabinet. However, there are instances where a 90° hinge is more appropriate, particularly if the cabinet door opens beside a wall or another restriction close to the cabinet. The flexibility of these hinges is impressive and installation is easy.

Adjustable Legs

Adjustable cabinet legs on the base cabinets, which are used extensively in this building system, change the traditional side design. In systems without the legs, the sides were longer and required a notch to provide the under-cabinet clearance called the toe kick space. When the side couldn't be seen, the traditional method was to build a base support frame of 2 × 4 lumber. That traditional method was strong, but gave rise to problems when the floor wasn't level. You had to shim the base frame support until you had a level surface, which was very time-consuming.

Drawer Glides

Another dramatic departure from the traditional North American style of cabinetry is the use of European drawer glides. These glides consist of two drawer runners and two side runners. You do not have to build hardwood drawer rails and inset drawer bottoms, which increases the design possibilities. In this building method, we use the 75-pound-rated bottom-mount drawer glide. The drawer body is built in the same method as an upper cabinet carcass (see chapter five). Drawer building will be detailed in chapter nine.

CHAPTER FOUR
Face Frame Cabinetry

THE BASIC BOX: AN OVERVIEW OF CONSTRUCTION

Years ago, building kitchen cabinets meant calculating the size of each cabinet, cutting the parts, determining if the cabinet was an end unit or middle-of-the-run unit and assembling each piece. It was time-consuming and slow. Today many cabinetmakers, both the small and large production shops, have adopted a systems approach to building kitchen cabinets.

European vs. North American Cabinets

Cabinets are sized in specific increments and built as a unit. In some European countries, kitchen cabinets are moved from house to house much like furniture, so a modular approach is important. The North American industry realized the value of this approach. The system offered flexibility with quality and could be incorporated with the high-quality North American-style cabinet by replacing the edge tape with a wooden face frame in the traditional style.

The Europeans perfected the "box" or unitized construction methods to a point where the frameless cabinet, often called the Euro-style kitchen cabinet, has become a popular option in North America. European design features such as the hidden hinge, bottom-mount drawer glides and adjustable cabinet legs are now an important part of the North American cabinetmaking industry.

This kitchen cabinet building system is based on that box-style construction. The techniques apply to cabinet carcasses and drawer assemblies. Think of the construction system in its basic form, and don't get confused with thinking in terms of the finished product. If you break the system down to the box concept—four sides and a bottom—you'll quickly understand and appreciate the simplicity of the construction methods.

Joinery

The joints are almost all butt joints, secured with 2″ screws designed specifically for particle board material. The strength of the butt joints is due in large part to the holding ability of these

Tip

Drill pilot holes for any joint that will be secured with particle core board (PCB) screws. This will prevent the PCB from splitting by allowing the screw to self-thread the hole. The pilot hole and screw combination is one of the most critical applications of this building style. Proper joint assembly will result in a long-lasting and very high quality cabinet.

Fig. 4-1

Butt-joined particle board and hardwood face frame

screws. They are installed in a predrilled pilot hole and, because of their design, thread the hole, providing an extremely strong joint. However, we can also use the many other high-quality methods available, such as biscuit, dowel and tenon joinery. Whichever joint you feel more comfortable with is perfectly acceptable.

Base and Upper Cabinets

I suggest that you use ⅝″-thick particle core board material as your standard. As discussed, it's strong and able to accommodate the loading capacity that kitchen cabinets are often required to handle. A full ⅝″-thick back should also be standard. It provides many advantages, including the elimination of cabinet mounting strips that are normally seen on the inside top and bottom of cabinets. You'll end up with a stronger cabinet that stays square, reducing the twisting and racking that sometimes occur during installation. The cabinet can be installed by screws into a stud wall anywhere through the back. Most importantly from a maintenance point of view, you never have to paint the wall behind the cabinet;

it is completely hidden. Both top and bottom cabinets are built with this full ⅝″ back board, making each unit extremely strong. After completing the installation, and after all the cabinets are secured to the wall as well as joined to each other, you'll have a very strong and stable unit. This strength helps keep doors properly aligned.

Make certain that all boards are cut square and to the proper dimensions. The two most critical boards in terms of dimension are the top and bottom, as they determine the inside width of the cabinet. The face frame must be installed on the cabinet face edge with the inside width of the face frame being slightly less than the inside width of the cabinet carcass. This ensures that the exposed edges of the PCB are fully covered and European hinges can be properly mounted. The face frame is built as an assembly, as is the cabinet carcass. Therefore, it's important that you pay close attention to accurately cutting the cabinet carcass top and bottom boards as well as the face frame rails.

The upper cabinet carcasses are built with five pieces of PCB: two sides, which are almost

Fig. 4-2

The ⅝″ cabinet back board makes the "box" very stable.

Fig. 4-3

Side view of an upper cabinet box (carcass)

Fig. 4-4

Side view of a basic cabinet box (carcass)

always drilled to accept the pins for adjustable shelves, a bottom and top piece, as well as an overlapping back piece. The sides are fastened to the bottom and top boards with a butt joint and secured with three PCB screws. The back forms the "bottom" of the box and is installed so it fully covers the edges. In reality, the bottom of the box is the back of the cabinet.

The standard upper cabinet carcass depth is 11¼″, made up of 10⅝″-wide sides, top and bottom plus the thickness of the applied back board. The total width increases to 12″ when a ¾″-thick wood face frame is installed. A 12″-deep upper cabinet with adjustable shelves is an industry standard. There are applications for deeper upper cabinets, which are easily built by simply increasing the depth of the sides as well as the top and bottom boards.

The upper cabinets over a fridge, stove and sink are usually reduced-height cabinets. All dimensions remain the same, with the exception of the sides and back board height.

Base Cabinet Differences

Standard base cabinets differ from upper cabinets in that they require only four boards. All you need are two sides, a bottom and a back. The top is not required because the countertop acts as the cabinet top. Sides are drilled to accept adjustable shelves only if required. Very often, base cabinets are fitted with pull-out shelves to provide accessible storage for pots and pans.

As with the uppers, the bottom board dimensions are the most critical because they will determine the inside dimensions of the cabinet carcass. All base cabinets, with a couple of exceptions, which we will discuss later, are constructed of ⅝″ melamine-coated PCB in the box style. Butt joints, pilot holes and PCB screws are used when building these cabinets. Additional screws are used for the butt joints, as the base cabinets are normally 24″ deep. You should use a 2″ PCB screw every six inches as your standard.

DRAWER CONSTRUCTION OVERVIEW

Drawer construction is sometimes very intimidating. Building drawers seems complicated and beyond the ability of the average do-it-yourselfer. In reality, it's a very simple process once you understand the basic box concept.

The drawers are constructed in the same fashion as the upper cabinets. You require two sides, a front, back and a bottom board. The drawer box is identical to the upper cabinet box, normally in smaller scale and used in a horizontal position. In place of the face frame, the exposed edges can be trimmed with ¼" hardwood strips and the bottom edges are covered with iron-on melamine tape. It's a simple construction method that produces a long-lasting drawer.

In this building system we use the bottom-mount drawer glide that is rated to carry a 75-pound load. Using ⅝" melamine-coated particle core board for the box parts, hardwood trim on the exposed PCB edges, melamine tape on the bottom edges, bottom-mounted drawer glides and a hardwood drawer front produces a very attractive and functional drawer. Drawer dimensions are determined by the width and height of the opening in the cabinet. With most bottom-mount drawer glides, the drawer carcass is 1" less in total width than the opening; all hardware comes with very specific installation instructions.

You'll soon see the strength of this box style of cabinet construction. The sides overlap the back and front board edges, and the bottom board completely covers the edges of one opening. If you cut your bottom board square, the drawer box will be square when it's installed.

Understanding the finished cabinet size relationship is also important. Cabinets are specific sizes so that industry-standard doors can be used

Fig. 4-5

Drawers are simply a box with bottom-mounted drawer glides.

Fig. 4-6

On a standard cabinet with 1"-wide stiles, the inside dimension is always 2" less than the total cabinet width.

to lower your cost. The standard cabinet uses a face frame with two 1"-wide stiles; therefore, the inside width of the carcass will be 2" less, allowing for proper hinge and door installation.

This may be a little unclear at this point, but as you will see, a high-quality building system that is complete, simple and flexible also allows you to quickly calculate your material needs.

THE FACE FRAME

Face frames are simply rectangular frames of wood consisting of stiles, which are the vertical members, and rails, which are the horizontal members. The purpose of this wooden frame is to cover the exposed edges of the cabinet carcass assembly. The frame, glued and nailed to the carcass edges, also provides additional strength to the cabinet.

This construction method, with the installation of hardwood cabinet doors, looks very traditional. The cabinet door covers all but ⅜″ of the stile. As discussed previously, we are using full-overlay Euro hidden hinges that allow the door a ⅝″ stile overlap. When cabinets are installed side by side, the face frames are joined with a 1¼″ screw through the edge to securely hold them in position. The resulting space or reveal between cabinet doors is ¾″.

The completed face frames are secured to the cabinet carcass, flush with the top of the cabinet, hanging ¾″ below the bottom of the cabinet, as illustrated in Figure 4-8. I secure the face frames to the carcass with glue and 2″ spiral finishing nails at 8″ centers. Pilot holes are a necessity prior to hammering in the nails. Countersink the nails, and use a wax stick matching the finished color of the cabinet wood to hide the holes.

Face Frame Corner Joints

The corner butt joints for the face frames can be glued and secured with two 2″ wood screws at each corner. Countersunk predrilled holes should be made prior to screw insertion. This creates a tight joint and allows for a ⅜″ wood filler plug to be placed in the screw hole should this cabinet be an end cabinet that requires hidden screw holes.

Fig. 4-7

Finishing exposed cabinet sides with ¼″ veneer ply and doorstop molding

Exposed Cabinet Sides

When the cabinet end will be exposed, use a 1⅜″ stile on the exposed end. This allows you to install a ¼″ wood veneer panel along with ¼″-thick molding. Wood plugs on the exposed stile are sanded smooth, giving the cabinet a professionally finished appearance. Remember to account for this added width, particularly with base cabinets. A standard 36″ base cabinet becomes 36⅜″ wide—an important consideration when calculating countertop length.

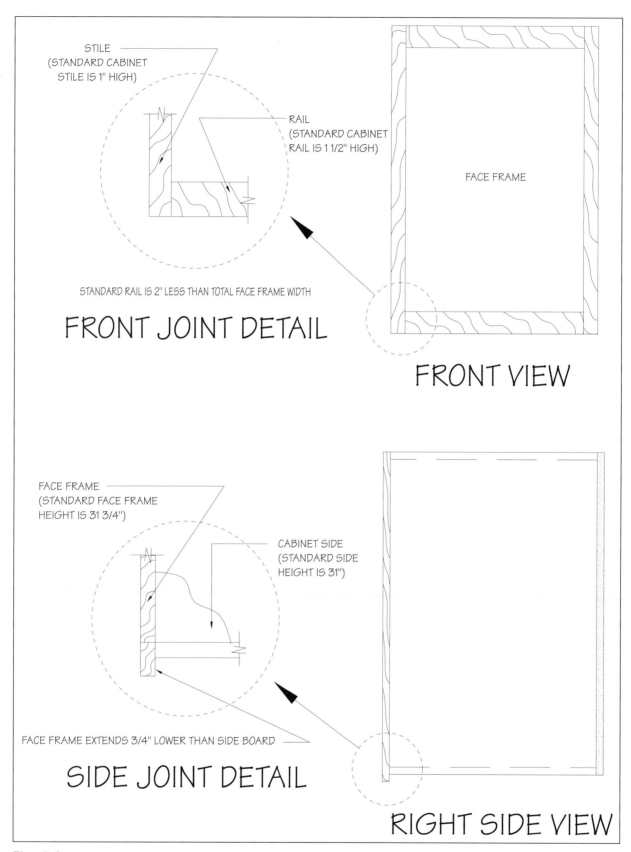

STILE
(STANDARD CABINET
STILE IS 1" HIGH)

RAIL
(STANDARD CABINET
RAIL IS 1 1/2" HIGH)

STANDARD RAIL IS 2" LESS THAN TOTAL FACE FRAME WIDTH

FRONT JOINT DETAIL

FACE FRAME

FRONT VIEW

FACE FRAME
(STANDARD FACE FRAME
HEIGHT IS 31 3/4")

CABINET SIDE
(STANDARD SIDE
HEIGHT IS 31")

FACE FRAME EXTENDS 3/4" LOWER THAN SIDE BOARD

SIDE JOINT DETAIL

RIGHT SIDE VIEW

Fig. 4-8

Standard face frame details for both upper and lower cabinets

Other Joinery Methods

Face frame joinery isn't limited to the butt joint and screws. Mortise-and-tenon joints, as well as the lap joint, can also be used very successfully when constructing the face frames.

A lap joint has one member overlapping the other. The simplest form is accomplished by using two equal-size rabbet joints. With glue and a few nails on the back side, this joint can be made very strong and attractive.

If you want to completely hide the joinery at the corner of the face frame, a mortise-and-tenon joint is by far the best choice. A tenon is cut on both ends of the rail and fitted into an open-end mortise on the stile. When using this joinery method be sure to account for the length of the tenons when calculating your rail length.

My preferences are the screwed butt joint and the mortise-and-tenon joint. However you're not limited to these suggested methods. Just about any good-quality joint, including dowel spline or biscuit joints, can be used to secure the face frame. It is really a matter of per-

sonal preference and one that you're most comfortable with. I'd suggest you experiment with a few alternatives to see which one is best suited to your needs and the equipment you have in your workshop.

Sizes

The following table details the face frame sizes for each of the standard cabinets. All face frames are ¾″-thick solid wood.

Standard face frames are 31¾″ high for both the upper and base cabinets. Special situations and cabinets that use shorter and wider stiles will be detailed in later chapters. However, a high percentage of your cabinets will use the standard rail and stile dimensions as described in the chart.

Face frames are constructed of the same wood as the doors; most common are red oak, cherry, birch and pine. The final finish of the face frame wood is normally the same as the final finish on the doors.

FACE FRAME SIZES

Cabinet Width	Two Stiles Width × Height	Two Rails Height × Length
12″	1″ × 31¾″	1½″ × 10″
15″	1″ × 31¾″	1½″ × 13″
18″	1″ × 31¾″	1½″ × 16″
21″	1″ × 31¾″	1½″ × 19″
24″	1″ × 31¾″	1½″ × 22″
27″	1″ × 31¾″	1½″ × 25″
30″	1″ × 31¾″	1½″ × 28″
33″	1″ × 31¾″	1½″ × 31″
36″	1″ × 31¾″	1½″ × 34″

Building the Face Frame

A high-quality ⅛″ drill in a ⅜″ carbide-tipped countersink assembly is an excellent drilling tool for the butt joint screws. The ⅛″ pilot hole in the hardwood is important, as is a nice, clean, well-defined hole for the wood filler plug. The edge of the stile will be visible on end-run cabinets, so their appearance is critical in achieving a professional-looking project.

The face frame is an important part of this building system for two reasons. First, it allows us to construct a cabinet with a frameless-style carcass that will look traditional. Second, it gives the cabinet tremendous strength and rigidity. The cabinet is very resistive to racking and twisting, so the doors tend to remain in proper alignment. It's important that you secure the face frame to the carcass edges with glue and nails.

As described earlier, I use good yellow polyvinyl acetate wood glue with 2″ spiral finishing nails that are countersunk and fill the holes with a wax stick. The nail holes, for the most part, will be hidden by the overlap of the cabinet door, so don't be afraid of putting in too many nails. As a wise old carpenter once said, better to have one nail too many than one too few.

Fig. 4-10

Fill the countersunk nail holes with a wax stick that will match the color of the finished wood.

Fig. 4-9

Securing the face frame to the carcass with glue and finishing nails

CHAPTER FIVE

Building Upper Cabinets

CONSTRUCTION NOTES

The standard upper cabinet is the most basic cabinet in this building system. As previously discussed, it consists of two sides, a top, a bottom and a back board. A wooden face frame is attached to the front of the carcass to complete the assembly. Figure 5-1 details a basic standard upper cabinet.

ADJUSTABLE SHELVES

Normally, upper cabinets contain two shelves. These are adjustable so that you can configure the cabinet to your particular requirements. The easiest and most effective method for installing adjustable shelves is to drill a series of holes at 2″ centers in the side boards prior to assembly. To eliminate measuring and layout when drilling holes, a simple jig can be constructed (see Figure 5-4). You can also use a piece of perforated pegboard as your jig.

Hole spacing for the shelf pins is entirely up to you. If you want more than the normal adjustment range, drill your holes at 1″ centers. The

Tip

A steel pin with a plastic coating works best for my needs. Many adjustable shelf pins are plastic only and tend to break under heavy loads.

Fig. 5-1

Upper cabinets are a very important part of your kitchen project. They are used as a storage area for dishware and food products. In many kitchens they are the most-used cabinets.

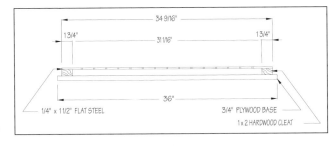

Fig. 5-2

A simple adjustable shelf-hole jig can be made from flat steel and metal as shown.

European standard for hole spacing is 32mm, or about 1¼", which should be suitable for the majority of situations and requirements.

Shelf support pins come in many shapes, sizes and colors. Select the type that is suitable to your needs prior to drilling the holes, as most pins require different hole diameters.

FACE FRAME CONSTRUCTION

The face frame, which is made out of hardwood, consists of two stiles and two rails. The stiles are the vertical members of the face frame and the rails are the horizontal members. In the standard cabinet, the stiles are 1" wide by 31¾" long; the rails are 1½" high and as wide as the inside dimension of the cabinet carcass. When we say that the face frame rail is as wide as the inside dimension of the cabinet carcass, we should qualify a point that might cause confusion later in the book. I make the top and bottom boards of the cabinet carcass ¹⁄₁₆" wider than the face frame rail. This ensures that the inside carcass dimension is just slightly larger than the inside dimension of the face frame, which guarantees the carcass edges will be fully covered. It gives us a small error factor in case any of our face frame rails are not perfectly cut to size. This extra width won't cause any problems when you are mounting the door hinges. All face frame material referred to in this book is assumed to be ¾" thick.

FULL BACK BOARD CONSTRUCTION BENEFITS

As briefly discussed earlier, the back on this cabinet design is a very important part of the system.

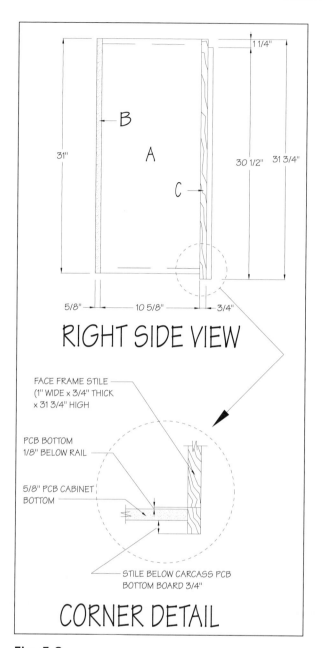

RIGHT SIDE VIEW

FACE FRAME STILE (1" WIDE x ¾" THICK x 31 3/4" HIGH

PCB BOTTOM 1/8" BELOW RAIL

5/8" PCB CABINET BOTTOM

STILE BELOW CARCASS PCB BOTTOM BOARD 3/4"

CORNER DETAIL

Fig. 5-3

The standard upper cabinet assembly showing the face frame-to-cabinet carcass (box) detail

It's unique in that quite a number of cabinets on the market use a ¼" veneer back board with two 1×2s for wall mounting. The ⅝" full backing gives the cabinet tremendous strength and rigidity. It also permits the screws used to attach the cabinet to the wall to be placed anywhere through the back board.

At this point I want to review the many advantages of full ⅝″ cabinet backing. First, mounting screws can be placed anywhere through the back board to hold cabinets securely to the wall. Second, the cabinet stays very rigid and is less likely to rack or twist during installation. Third, the wall behind the cabinet is fully covered and never needs painting. And finally, the back board, if cut square, will cause the cabinet carcass to be square after it's secured.

After building your first cabinet, try to twist it from side to side and take notice of the movement. Compare that with cabinets that have ¼″ back boards or those that use two strips of wood as wall anchor boards, and you will see the remarkable difference.

CARCASS CONSTRUCTION

A strong carcass that is almost maintenance free, because we are using ⅝″ melamine-coated PCB, and that is functional, with options such as adjustable shelves and without a center stile blocking the cabinet space, is a very desirable product. It's fine to have great-looking cabinets on the exterior, but we also want to achieve a high degree of quality within the interior spaces.

The sides or gable ends of the cabinet perform very important functions. Primarily, they define the height of the cabinet box and give it strength. The sides also support the European hidden hinges and are drilled for the shelf support pins. Also, in this particular cabinet style, the face frame is nailed onto the side edges as well as the top and bottom board edges.

The bottom and top boards of the cabinet carcass in conjunction with the sides form the box shape of the cabinet. More importantly though, the bottom and top boards define the interior width of the carcass. It is very important that care is taken to cut these two boards accurately and square. Interior width accuracy is important because the doors and the resulting door overlay are calculated based on the inside dimensions of the cabinet. This measurement determines combined door width, hinge style and individual door width. Obviously, if the bottom and top boards are not cut accurately and square, as well as equal to each other, the cabinet will not be square and will cause problems with door fitting and operation.

Accuracy in cutting of the cabinet pieces is important and cannot be stressed too often. Take your time and double-check your measurements. Correctly cut boards will turn the assembly tasks into a very simple process.

Cabinet sides are cut to a length of 31″, and the face frame stiles are cut at 31¾″. This is done so the face frame hangs ¾″ below the carcass bottom. This feature gives a little flexibility when assembling cabinets and hides the edges of under-cabinet finish boards that will be applied. Standard doors are 30½″ high and mounted flush with the bottom of the face frame so that 1¼″ will be left at the top of the cabinet for installation of edge molding.

Standard upper cabinet doors are mounted using European-style hidden hinges. A 35mm-diameter hole is drilled in the door, and the other end of the hinge is attached to the carcass side. Initially, I was a little intimidated by these hinges. Now, after using them for ten years or more, I feel that they are the best thing that happened to cabinet door hardware. They are strong, fully adjustable in three directions, available in a variety of opening configurations and virtually maintenance free. They are so dependable that some of the manufacturers guarantee them for life. Installation, although appearing somewhat complicated, is a very simple process.

Standard upper and base cabinets, as detailed, form the building blocks to the design.

Knowing the design and terminology and understanding the reasons for the sizes of the parts will allow you to adapt these cabinets to any special situation.

You will get to a point, after studying this design, that will allow you to plan, order materials and list your finished cut sizes, as well as order industry-standard doors or make your own doors, because you understand the size relationship of each part of the cabinet.

Cutting Upper Cabinet Parts

Standard upper cabinet size and construction practices will be addressed first. The following table is a cut list with all the carcass component sizes based on $5/8''$ melamine-coated particle core board material. I normally use the white melamine-coated material because of its availability and the "clean" interior look it gives to the cabinets. Also, all the accessories, such as towel racks, drawer slides and lazy susan assemblies, are readily available in white as a stock item from most suppliers.

In addition to the pieces for each upper carcass assembly, you will require a minimum of two shelf boards for each cabinet. The shelves for the upper cabinets are always $10\frac{5}{8}''$ deep and $\frac{1}{16}''$ less, in total width, than the top or bottom carcass boards. For example, in the case of a 30"-wide standard upper, you would need two shelf boards at $10\frac{5}{8}''$ deep by 28" wide.

It may appear a little strange that some of the dimensions are as close as $\frac{1}{16}''$, such as in the case of the top and bottom carcass boards. I calculate it that way to ensure that the interior dimension of the cabinet is just slightly wider than the inside dimension of the cabinet face frame. This guarantees the face frame will completely cover the exposed edges of the PCB carcass.

The back board width is slightly wider than required for another reason. If you take the 30" cabinet as an example and add the bottom board width of $28\frac{1}{16}''$ plus the combined thickness of both sides (2 @ $\frac{5}{8}''$ equals $1\frac{1}{4}''$), you have a total of $29\frac{5}{16}''$. The back board dimension in the chart for the 30" cabinet is $29\frac{1}{2}''$, obviously too wide. However, there is some slight thick-

UPPER CABINET CUT LIST

Upper Cabinet	Two Sides	Top and Bottom	One Back
12"	$10\frac{5}{8}'' \times 31''$	$10\frac{5}{8}'' \times 10\frac{1}{16}''$	$11\frac{1}{2}'' \times 31''$
15"	$10\frac{5}{8}'' \times 31''$	$10\frac{5}{8}'' \times 13\frac{1}{16}''$	$14\frac{1}{2}'' \times 31''$
18"	$10\frac{5}{8}'' \times 31''$	$10\frac{5}{8}'' \times 16\frac{1}{16}''$	$17\frac{1}{2}'' \times 31''$
21"	$10\frac{5}{8}'' \times 31''$	$10\frac{5}{8}'' \times 19\frac{1}{16}''$	$20\frac{1}{2}'' \times 31''$
24"	$10\frac{5}{8}'' \times 31''$	$10\frac{5}{8}'' \times 22\frac{1}{16}''$	$23\frac{1}{2}'' \times 31''$
27"	$10\frac{5}{8}'' \times 31''$	$10\frac{5}{8}'' \times 25\frac{1}{16}''$	$26\frac{1}{2}'' \times 31''$
30"	$10\frac{5}{8}'' \times 31''$	$10\frac{5}{8}'' \times 28\frac{1}{16}''$	$29\frac{1}{2}'' \times 31''$
33"	$10\frac{5}{8}'' \times 31''$	$10\frac{5}{8}'' \times 31\frac{1}{16}''$	$32\frac{1}{2}'' \times 31''$
36"	$10\frac{5}{8}'' \times 31''$	$10\frac{5}{8}'' \times 34\frac{1}{16}''$	$35\frac{1}{2}'' \times 31''$

ness variation in material from different production runs and manufacturers. To eliminate problems, the back board is cut a little wider and then trimmed flush with a router bit after installation on the carcass.

Complete coverage of the carcass edges on the back of the cabinet is important. As previously mentioned, this ⅝″ back board adds strength and stability to the cabinets. The back board, secured to the carcass edges with 2″ particle board screws at 4″ centers, creates a free-standing, extremely strong modular unit. The cabinets are secured to the wall by screwing through this back board. The upper cabinets are actually hung by screwing through the back board and into the wall studs. The base cabinet back board is anchored to the wall to stabilize the cabinet position only, since most of the base cabinet weight is taken on the adjustable legs. And since it fully covers the carcass, screws can be placed in any location on the board.

The back board is an asset because, unlike some cabinets on the market without a full ⅝″ back, the interior of the cabinet is virtually maintenance free. You don't have to paint the wall behind the cabinet. However, the major advantages are structural stability and ease of installation for the cabinetmaker.

BUILDING THE STANDARD UPPER CABINET

In the case of upper cabinets, first ensure that all PCB and face frame components are accurately cut to size.

1 Drill Shelf Holes
Drill the holes in each side board for the adjustable shelves if the cabinet is to be so equipped. During assembly, ensure that the top-to-top relationship of each side is maintained, particularly if the holes are started at different distances from the top and bottom of the side.

2 Join the Sides
Fasten one side to the edge of the bottom board, making sure the joint is square and flush. Drill a ⅛″ countersunk pilot hole for each of the three 2″ PCB screws. Do not overtighten or apply so much force to the screws that they strip their threaded hole. Take care as well to drill the pilot hole so that it's in the center of the edge on the board you are fastening the side to; in this case, the bottom board of the carcass. Connect the remaining three corner joints in the same manner.

Fig. 5-4
Shelf-pin holes can be drilled with a homemade jig.

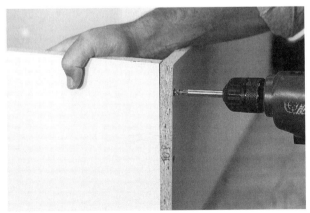

Fig. 5-5
Fasten the sides to the bottom and top boards.

3 Check the Size

For purposes of verification at this point, referencing a 30″ upper cabinet as an example, you should have a four-sided box with inside dimensions of 28¹⁄₁₆″ wide (the width of the bottom and top carcass boards) by 29¾″ high (the length of the side minus the thickness of the top and bottom carcass boards).

4 Attach the Back

Attach the back board to the carcass, flush with three edges of the box. This will square the carcass. Remember, the back board is intentionally cut wider to accommodate thickness variances in the PCB material. As discussed earlier, you will have one side with a slight overhang. Secure the back to the carcass frame using 2″ PCB screws at 4″ centers. Use a marking gauge to draw lines ⁵⁄₁₆″ in from the edges as a guide for the pilot holes. As one side of the back has a slight overhang, take this into account when you are marking your guide lines on that side.

5 Trim the Back Board

After securing the back, flush-trim the overhang with a flush-trim bit in a router. This joint will not be seen, so I use an old carbide router bit as the PCB material tends to dull cutting tools.

6 Check the Square

At this point, ensure that the holes for the adjustable shelf pins are in correct side-to-side relationship with each other and that the carcass is square. Either measure the diagonals of the carcass and verify that they are equal or use a framing square on the inside of the carcass.

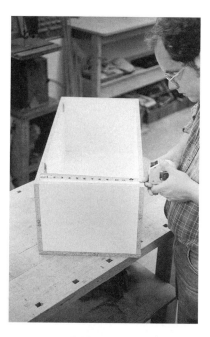

Fig. 5-6
Check that the inside dimensions are correct.

Fig. 5-7
Attach the back board flush on three sides.

Fig. 5-8
After securing four sides of the back, trim carefully with a flush-trim router bit.

7 Build the Face Frame

Assemble the face frame as discussed earlier. With reference to a 30″ upper cabinet, verify that the outside measurement of the face frame is 30″ wide by 31¾″ long. The stiles should be 1″ wide, and the rails should be 1½″ high.

8 Install the Face Frame

Apply glue to the four carcass edges and place the outside face frame top edge flush with the outside top edge of the carcass. The face frame should fully cover the carcass edges; it should, in fact, be slightly smaller on the inside dimension vs. the inside dimension of the carcass. The carcass bottom and top are cut ¹⁄₁₆″ larger than the face frame rails to guarantee full carcass edge coverage by the face frame. Divide the difference between the two inside edges. Secure the top corner of the face frame to the carcass body using 2″ spiral finish nails in a pilot hole slightly smaller than the nail thickness. Drill the pilot hole so that it centers, as much as possible, on the PCB edge. Secure the other top corner so that the top outside of the face frame is flush with the top outside edge of the carcass. Secure the bottom two corners, keeping the slight overhang of the face frame inside the carcass maintained equally on both sides. Install the remaining nails at 8″ centers, maintaining the overhang. The bottom rail should hang below the cabinet carcass by ¾″, and the sides of the face frame should extend ⅜″ beyond each side of the carcass. The inside edge of the bottom rail will be slightly above the bottom board.

9 Finish Detail

Set the nails below the surface and fill the holes with a wax stick that will match the finished color of the cabinet wood. Doors and shelves can be installed at this point.

Fig. 5-9
Check that the carcass box is square by measuring the diagonals. Equal distances mean your "box" is square.

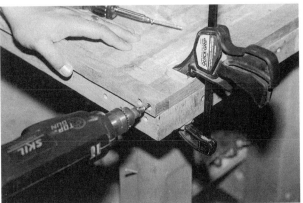

Fig. 5-10
One method of face frame joinery is a butt joint using glue and 2″ screws in a piloted countersunk hole.

Fig. 5-11
Secure the face frame to the carcass with glue and 2″ spiral finishing nails.

24″ UPPER CORNER CABINET ASSEMBLY

An upper corner cabinet with a lazy susan assembly is a very popular and useful addition in a kitchen renovation project. It's very common to plan for corner cabinets as most kitchens, with the exception of the galley style, have a corner wall.

This cabinet is called a 24″ upper corner because it takes up 24″ on each wall of a corner. The face is at a 45° angle to the cabinets on either side. Dead space, often found in corner wall cabinets, is minimized by the installation of a two-shelf lazy susan assembly.

This cabinet is probably the most difficult unit to build in the system. Face frame members have to be cut at 22½° angles so the two parts of each stile form a 45° angle. However, don't let the construction details intimidate you: It's easier than it appears.

The following is a cut list for the standard 24″ upper corner cabinet with an 18″ round, two-shelf lazy susan unit.

Refer to Figure 5-13 for assembly and angle-cutting details, as well as reference and detail for the face frame cutting and assembly.

Like all the other cabinets, cutting the boards to their proper size is important. Cut the top and bottom boards to the size stated in the table, leaving the angle cut until you are ready to assemble the pieces. As illustrated in the table, pay particular attention to the back board cut sizes. One back is ⅝″ wider to allow for the required overlap of the boards during assembly.

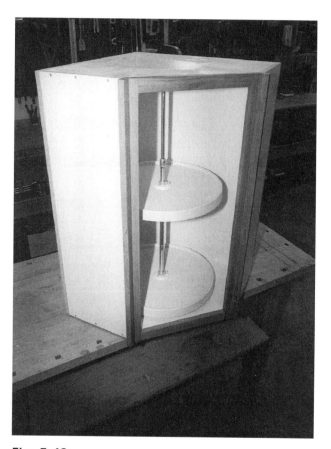

Fig. 5-12

The upper corner cabinet looks complicated to build but it is actually easy to construct.

24″ UPPER CORNER CABINET CUT LIST

Type	Required	Size	Comments
Side	2	10⅝″ × 31″	
Top and Bottom	2	22⅛″ × 22⅛″	Cut as illustrated in drawing
Back	1	22¾″ × 31″	
Back	1	23⅜″ × 31″	

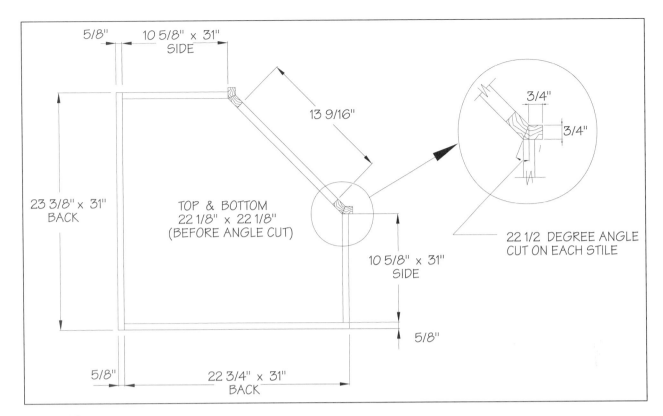

Fig. 5-13
The 24" upper corner cabinet showing cut sizes and face frame details

1 Cut the Parts

There are six particle core boards required for this cabinet; cut as indicated. This cabinet is almost always fitted with a two-shelf 18" lazy susan assembly and, therefore, holes for adjustable shelves are not required.

2 Assemble the Boards

Assemble the boards as shown in Figure 5-13 and ensure all joints are square and secure. Drill ⅛" countersunk pilot holes and use 2" PCB screws at 4" centers.

3 Join the Face Frame

Cut the six wood parts for the face frame assembly and assemble as indicated. This face frame can be a little difficult to assemble; however, the use of angle clamps will aid in holding the stiles in place while they are glued and screwed to each other. Cut the parts as close as possible to the indicated angle and assemble with care.

4 Install the Face Frame

Glue and nail the face frame to the carcass as shown in Figure 5-14. Install the face frame so that the outside top of the face frame is flush with the outside top of the corner carcass.

The inside surface of the stiles are not flush with the sides, as in the other cabinets, so a special face frame hinge plate is used to secure the hinges and door for this cabinet.

Fig. 5-14

Installing the face frame on the upper corner cabinet

OVER-THE-STOVE UPPER CABINETS

Stove cabinets are not as large as standard upper cabinets because a range hood is normally mounted under the cabinet. Also, greater clearance between the stove and the upper cabinet is required to properly work at the stove.

I normally install a 30"-wide, 19¼"-high cabinet with 18"-high doors. These measurements are for cabinets over standard-size stoves. I use a 30"-wide cabinet with ½" added to the adjoining stiles of the cabinets on either side. I want the space between the base units on each side of the stove to be 31", and the wider upper stiles allow me to accomplish this when the base cabinets are lined up with the uppers. I can then overhang my countertop by ⅜" on each base cabinet beside the stove, which allows for a maximum opening, between the countertop ends, of 30¼" for the stove. Widening the cabinet stiles on the right and left of the stove upper permits countertop overhang and allows for proper clearance of the stove.

You can custom design any size over-the-stove cabinet you need following the design rules. Refer back to the industry-standard door sizes when designing custom cabinets. The basic rules of the inside width of the face frame equalling the inside width of the cabinet carcass, the face frame being ¾" greater than the cabinet carcass in total height, and the doors being 1¼" less than the face frame height determine your cabinet dimensions.

The stove cabinet I normally use follows the

Tip

Take note of the width of the range hood prior to finalizing your cut list. Most, if not all, hoods are the required 30" wide, as it's an accepted industry standard. However, there may be variances from manufacturer to manufacturer and it pays to check up front. Also, range hoods with built-in features such as microwaves are becoming more popular and, although they should conform to the standard dimensions, it would be worth checking.

rules. The face frame is 19¼" high, with two 14½"-wide by 18"-high doors, the inside carcass width is 28", and the sides are 18½" high. The 28" inside cabinet width plus the total width of the two 1" stiles equals a cabinet that is 30" wide.

OVER-THE-FRIDGE UPPER CABINETS

There are two sizes of cabinets that I use as over-the-fridge cabinets. You have a choice based on your requirements.

The majority of refrigerators on the market today are 31" to 32" wide, so my normal cabinet width for either style is 33". Refrigerators are approximately 65" high, leaving a clearance of about 20" for a cabinet above the appliance. I use a standard maximum cabinet height of 85", made up of a 36" base unit and countertop height, plus 18" countertop surface to the bottom of the upper cabinet distance and 31" upper cabinet height. I want the top of the fridge cabinet even with the uppers at that 85" height.

Your choice depends on how much clearance you would like between the bottom of the cabinet and the top of the fridge. A 17¼" cabinet with 16"-high standard doors will leave a 2¾" space, and a 14¼" cabinet with 13"-high standard doors will leave a 5¾" space.

Follow the standard rules for building either one of these cabinets, and install an adjustable shelf in both the over-the-stove and over-the-fridge cabinets. If these shelves are not required you can always remove them.

Calculating parts for any cabinet can be easily accomplished by working backwards from the door dimension. The over-the-fridge cabinet, called a 17¼"-high upper, takes 16"-high doors. We know, based on the standard design rules,

that there is a 1¼" space above the door; therefore our face frame is 17¼" high. Each door is 16" wide because of our rule that the face frame is 1" wider than the combined width of the doors on the two-door 33" fridge cabinet.

Since the stiles on a regular face frame are 1" wide, the bottom and top board of this cabinet must be 31" wide. Also, the standard face frame hangs ¾" below the cabinet bottom and is flush with the top, so our sides must be 16½" high. The back board is the height of the sides and as wide as the bottom or top board plus the thickness of the two sides.

Cabinet depth on this upper is a matter of personal choice. Some people like the look of a recessed cabinet (standard 12" depth) over the fridge, while others want a cabinet flush with the appliance door. Simply adjust the depth of the sides, top and bottom boards, taking into account the thickness of the face frame and the cabinet door, to get the desired total cabinet depth.

OVER-THE-SINK UPPER CABINETS

Clearance is required when working at the sink; therefore, over-the-sink cabinets, when installed, are not normally full-height cabinets. Standard widths are used, a 36"-wide cabinet in most cases; however, the height is the same as the over-the-stove cabinet at 19¼".

This reduced-height sink upper is by no means a hard-and-fast design rule. I have used both standard full-height and reduced-height uppers over the sink. I will usually install under-cabinet lighting, as discussed in chapter eight, on this cabinet. In kitchens where a window is not over the sink cabinet, task lighting is a very practical feature.

CHAPTER SIX
Building Base Cabinets

CONSTRUCTION NOTES

The standard base cabinet, as shown, differs from the standard upper cabinet in two areas. The main differences are the lack of a carcass top board and the addition of adjustable legs.

There are two sides measuring 31″ high, the same as the upper cabinet sides. However, the depth of these pieces is greater, as the normal overall base cabinet depth in the industry is about 24″. The finished cut size of the sides is 31″ × 22⅛″. Adding the thickness of the ⅝″ back and the ¾″ face frame gives a total cabinet depth of 23½″. Installed standard ¾″-thick doors bring the total depth to 24¼″.

There is no top board, as the kitchen countertop covers the base cabinet. The countertop is secured to the base cabinet by means of screws and right-angle clips. This method, along with the face frame, gives the installed base cabinet its strength and rigidity. I use ¾″ × ¾″ metal right-angle clips: two per side, two on the back board and one in the center of the top face frame rail. The countertop is secured with two ⅝″ screws through each right-angle clip.

Metal right-angle clips have many uses and advantages. Primarily, the clip will not allow the ⅝″ screw to drive through the countertop material. If you've ever driven a screw through your new countertop during installation, you'll appreciate this safety feature.

Adjustable cabinet legs are installed, replac-

Fig. 6-1

Bases can be sink cabinets, drawer banks or drawer-over-door, with built-in adjustable shelves, pull-outs and garbage containers. Some base units are constructed to suit specific needs, while others are used for general storage.

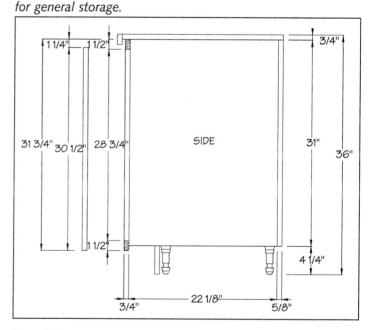

Fig. 6-2

The standard base cabinet has a full-height door and one full-depth adjustable shelf.

ing the base frame that was quite common with older-style kitchens. These legs allow for easy installation and hold the toe kick board by means of special clips called plinth clips.

The adjustable cabinet legs are very popular and can be purchased at a kitchen hardware supply store. The total cost of the legs for each cabinet is greater than the cost of the material for a wood base. However, the building time for the base when added to the difficulty of cabinet installation justifies the extra few dollars. Cabinet legs are, in my opinion, one of the positive features that the North American industry has adopted from European cabinetry. The ease of installation, even in the most difficult situations, is remarkable. Most legs adjust from 3½″ to 4½″ in height. In effect, the kitchen floor would have to be out of level by more than 1″ before the legs required shims. Some of the additional benefits of plastic cabinet legs are shown in Figure 6-5.

The bottom board determines the inside carcass width and must be cut accurately and squarely. The back board serves the same function as the upper cabinet back board, allowing screws to be placed where necessary to secure the cabinet to the wall. It also ensures that the cabinet carcass is square.

The face frame, as in the upper cabinet, consists of two stiles and two rails. The stiles are 1″ wide × 31¾″ long, and the rails are 1½″ high by the interior cabinet dimension width. The standard base door at 30½″ high is mounted with European-type hinges in the same fashion as the upper doors.

The base units are a box design, like the uppers, with a couple of minor changes. However, the side heights are identical, as are the face frame and door dimensions. As you will see, this uniformity in design is a real benefit when cutting cabinet pieces, calculating door requirements and planning the cutting lists.

Fig. 6-3

Metal angle clips secure the countertop to the base.

Fig. 6-4

Adjustable legs are secured with special screws through the base board.

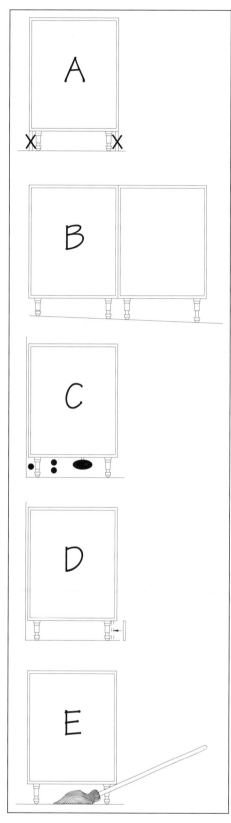

Fig. 6-5

Adjustable cabinet legs provide many positive benefits for the kitchen cabinetmaker.

Base cabinets are multi-function units. They are equipped with adjustable shelves, pull-out shelf assemblies, drawers or other special features such as trash and recycling containers. Holes for the adjustable shelves are drilled in the carcass sides by the same method and with the same jig assembly as the standard upper cabinets. Drawers and pull-outs are easily installed using the European bottom-mount drawer glide hardware.

Accessories for kitchen cabinet base units are very popular items in most building supply centers. Each year seems to bring more and more optional equipment that can be installed, such as pull-out wire baskets, towel racks, laundry hampers and double, triple and quadruple recycling bin systems, as well as flip-out ironing boards and workcenter platforms. You won't be at a loss when looking for interesting accessories for your new kitchen cabinets.

Once again, the most critical area is the accurate cutting of the cabinet parts. The sides must be cut square and to a correct uniform dimension. The bottom board's width must be accurate, as it determines the inside width of the cabinet. As in the case of the upper cabinets, the bottom board is $1/16''$ wider than the face frame rail to ensure complete coverage of the carcass edges.

CUTTING BASE CABINET PARTS

A table of sizes (cut list) for the PCB pieces required to assemble the standard base cabinets is shown on page 67.

If your design requires adjustable shelves, you'll need to calculate that material into your plan. Shelves for the base unit are $22\frac{1}{8}''$ deep and $1/16''$ less than the width of the base bottom board. As discussed earlier, the $\frac{1}{16}''$ added width measurement of the bottom is to ensure that the inside dimension of the cabinet is just slightly larger than the inside dimension of the face frame so that the carcass edges will be fully covered by the face frame. With respect to the standard base cabinets, a top board is not required, as the kitchen countertop will cover this area.

It should be noted at this point that prior to cutting the PCB material, you should verify that it is indeed $\frac{5}{8}''$ thick. I have seen variances in this product, even from the same manufacturer, that could cause you some trouble. Take the variances, if any, into account when creating your cut list.

BUILDING THE STANDARD BASE CABINET

Base cabinet assembly uses the same basic procedures as were used in building the upper cabinets; however, there are a few minor differences that will be detailed.

1 Drill Shelf Holes

Drill holes in each side for the adjustable shelf pins if the cabinet is to be so equipped. If adjustable shelves are to be installed, ensure that the top-to-top relationship of the sides is maintained.

2 Install Legs

Install the adjustable legs on the cabinet base board using the screws and installation techniques suggested by the manufacturer of the legs you are using. Generally, the legs are attached by means of holes drilled through the base board. The screw is then threaded into the leg, with the base board sandwiched between the screw and the leg. Set the legs $3\frac{1}{2}''$ back from the front edge of the base board to allow setback for the toe kick space. Drill the holes so that the leg will extend beyond the back and both side edges by $\frac{5}{8}''$. This will allow the sides and the back board to rest on the leg flanges, providing additional support for the cabinet. Part of the loads placed on the cabinet will be transferred through the legs to the floor.

BASE CABINET CUT LIST

Base Cabinet	Two Sides	One Bottom	One Back
12"	$22\frac{1}{8}'' \times 31''$	$22\frac{1}{8}'' \times 10\frac{1}{16}''$	$11\frac{1}{2}'' \times 31''$
15"	$22\frac{1}{8}'' \times 31''$	$22\frac{1}{8}'' \times 13\frac{1}{16}''$	$14\frac{1}{2}'' \times 31''$
18"	$22\frac{1}{8}'' \times 31''$	$22\frac{1}{8}'' \times 16\frac{1}{16}''$	$17\frac{1}{2}'' \times 31''$
21"	$22\frac{1}{8}'' \times 31''$	$22\frac{1}{8}'' \times 19\frac{1}{16}''$	$20\frac{1}{2}'' \times 31''$
24"	$22\frac{1}{8}'' \times 31''$	$22\frac{1}{8}'' \times 22\frac{1}{16}''$	$23\frac{1}{2}'' \times 31''$
27"	$22\frac{1}{8}'' \times 31''$	$22\frac{1}{8}'' \times 25\frac{1}{16}''$	$26\frac{1}{2}'' \times 31''$
30"	$22\frac{1}{8}'' \times 31''$	$22\frac{1}{8}'' \times 28\frac{1}{16}''$	$29\frac{1}{2}'' \times 31''$
33"	$22\frac{1}{8}'' \times 31''$	$22\frac{1}{8}'' \times 31\frac{1}{16}''$	$32\frac{1}{2}'' \times 31''$
36"	$22\frac{1}{8}'' \times 31''$	$22\frac{1}{8}'' \times 34\frac{1}{16}''$	$35\frac{1}{2}'' \times 31''$

3 Assemble the Box

Fasten the sides and back to the base board as detailed in the upper cabinet assembly instructions (chapter five).

4 Install the Face Frame

Install the face frame in the same manner as detailed in the upper cabinet assembly instructions (chapter five). The difference in this step is that the base carcass does not have a top board; therefore, the side tops can move easily. Make sure the top edge of the face frame is flush with the top corner edge of the side, and that the inside edge of the face frame is slightly past the inside edge of the side. Secure that corner with glue and a nail and then secure the other top corner. Fasten the bottom corners, maintaining the inside face frame overhang (approximately $\frac{1}{32}''$); then secure the face frame to the carcass with 2″ finishing nails at 8″ centers. The face frame should extend past the bottom of the carcass base board by $\frac{3}{4}''$, and the face frame sides should be $\frac{3}{8}''$ past the outside of each side.

5 Attach Countertop Clips

At this point, countertop clips are installed flush with the top and back edges of the carcass. Two per side, spaced equally around the top perimeter, are required. Clips are secured with $\frac{5}{8}''$ screws and will be used to fasten the countertop in place.

6 Finish Details

Set the face frame nails and fill the holes, trim the back board overhang and verify the cabinet is square. The cabinet is now ready for doors, drawers and/or shelves.

Fig. 6-6

Most cabinet legs are installed with a screw through the base board. Follow instructions supplied by the manufacturer for the legs you purchase.

Fig. 6-7

Countertop clips are attached, two per side and two on the back board.

36″ CORNER BASE CABINET

One of the most popular and effective storage options for kitchens is the 36″ corner base cabinet equipped with a 32″ pie-cut, two-shelf lazy susan assembly. This cabinet eliminates the lower dead zone in base cabinets where two cabinets meet in the corner. That four square feet of space is often ignored. Unless you have a kitchen the size of a tennis court, that space is very valuable real estate.

A two-shelf rotating lazy susan assembly can be purchased at most major kitchen hardware stores. Installation is a very simple matter with the supplied instructions. Major manufacturers such as Rev-A-Shelf Inc. produce a very high-quality assembly that will last many years.

The following is a cut list for the standard 36″ corner base unit normally equipped with a 32″ pie-cut, two-shelf lazy susan assembly.

Refer to Figure 6-8 for assembly and angle-cutting details, as well as reference and detail for the face frame cutting and assembly.

36″ CORNER BASE CABINET CUT LIST

Type	Required	Size	Comments
Side	2	22⅛″ × 31″	
Back	2	22⅝″ × 31″	
Back	1	18″ × 31″	Angle cut as illustrated in Figure 6-8
Bottom	1	33⅜″ × 33⅜″	Cut as illustrated in Figure 6-8

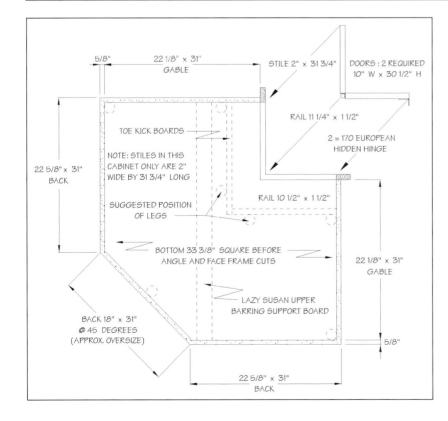

Fig. 6-8

The corner base with lazy susan is an ideal cabinet for maximizing the space where base cabinets meet in the corner.

BUILDING THE CORNER BASE CABINET

The following steps describe the assembly process.

1 Cut the Parts
There are six PCB pieces, as indicated in Figure 6-8 and in the cut list table. Accurately cut the pieces as detailed. Do not cut the angles on the 18″×31″ back board at this time. I recommend that you cut it with straight cuts to the stated 18″×31″ size.

2 Install the Legs
Install the cabinet legs in the positions as indicated in Figure 6-8. Maintain the 3½″ setback from the front edges of the cabinet. Remember that this setback is required for toe kick spacing on all the base cabinets. Position the other legs so that they will extend out ⅝″ from the edge of the base board to aid in supporting the cabinet sides.

3 Assemble the Parts
Assemble the cabinet boards as shown, leaving the 18″×31″ back board until all others are secured.

4 Fit the Angled Back
Measure the opening for the back board and fit the back by cutting 45° angles on each side.

5 Install the Face Frame
Cut and assemble the face frame as indicated and install so that the inside faces of the sides are flush with the inside surface of the face frame stiles.

Fig. 6-9
The angled back on the 36″ corner base makes it easier to move the finished cabinet through doorways.

6 Install Angle Clips
Install the angle clips, two per side, so that the countertop can be secured.

7 Install the Lazy Susan Support
A board must be installed across the center of the cabinet, as shown in Figure 6-8, to support the lazy susan bearing assembly. This cabinet is now ready for the 32″ pie-cut lazy susan and doors.

Tip

It may be helpful the first time you build one of these cabinets to angle-cut the back board so that it's a little larger and trial fit the back. Continue cutting the back board slightly smaller after each trial fit until it's perfect.

DRAWER-OVER-DOOR BASE CABINETS

One popular base cabinet is the drawer-over-door unit. The large drawer, particularly in a cabinet such as the 30″ base unit, is a very useful addition to most kitchens. This cabinet style is also used when a counter cooktop is installed. In that circumstance, a false drawer front is permanently attached to hide the cooktop mechanism when the doors are opened.

The interior of the cabinet, behind the doors, can be fitted with either a pull-out or an adjustable shelf.

Construction Notes

Construction procedures for this cabinet are identical to the standard base cabinet, with an added rail piece to cover the space between the door and drawer. The general design rule that applies is maintaining the 30½″ overall height so that we have the 1¼″ reveal at the top of the face frame. As previously discussed, our standard door height is 30½″ for full-door cabinets. When we construct a drawer-over-door cabinet, or any other combination cabinet, we want to maintain that height so that all doors and drawers are at the same level. Maintaining this uniform line is visually pleasing, especially with base cabinets. The combination of a 23½″ door and a 6¾″-high drawer face plus the ¼″ space between them gives us the required 30½″ height.

Drawer construction using the ⅝″ melamine PCB box method mounted on European bottom-mount drawer glides will be detailed in chapter nine. Door installation is the same as with all other doors, except we are using a 23½″-high

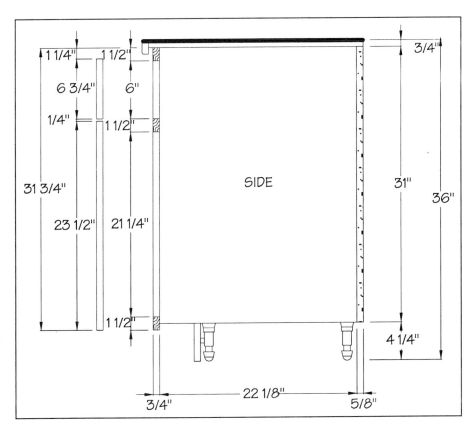

Fig. 6-10

The drawer-over-door base is a good way to gain extra drawer space. In some kitchens, many of the base cabinets are built in this fashion.

industry-standard-size door. If we use the 30″ base cabinet as an example, we would require two doors 23½″ high × 14½″ wide. The drawer face would be 6¾″ high × 29⅟₁₆″ wide. The drawer face width is a combination of the widths of the two doors plus a gap allowance between the two doors of ⅟₁₆″.

In the many of my kitchen projects, drawer faces are made from solid 1″ × 8″ hardwood. I decided on this method for a number of reasons, primarily because 1″ × 8″ lumber is dressed to ¾″ × 7¼″ so you won't have to be concerned with edge-joining boards. This reduces the time and cost required to manufacture the cabinets. Cabinet door style will determine the amount of work necessary to produce a compatible drawer face. In most cases, I use a router to apply a round-over or cove detail to the drawer edge. This method will produce a very good-looking drawer face for almost all of your applications.

There may be an occasion when you want a very fancy and intricate drawer face. In those instances you can order faces to match your door style from the door supplier. However, the cost per drawer face increases and you may want to compare the costs, particularly if you have quite a few drawers to build.

FOUR-DRAWER BASE CABINETS

Just about every kitchen has at least one of the four-drawer base cabinets. They are primarily used as a cutlery center and are often located near the sink and dishwasher.

The cabinet is nothing more than a standard base unit fitted with extra rails to hide the gaps between the drawers. As shown in Figure 6-12, there are some special spacing and rail-size considerations so that the 30½″ overall door,

drawer/door or multiple-drawer height is maintained.

Construct the face frame using the dimensions shown in Figure 6-12. There are a total of five rails which, when installed, will divide the face frame so that there are four drawer openings. Rails are cut at 31¾″ long and are 2″ less in width than the outside face frame dimension. Fasten each rail with glue and two 2″ screws. Counterbore the screw holes so that they can be filled with wood plugs if this cabinet is to be used as an open end-run cabinet.

Using a 30″ four-drawer base cabinet as an example, and standard ¾″-thick wood, this face frame would require two stiles 1″ wide × 31¾″ long, three rails 2″ wide × 28″ long, one rail 1¾″ wide × 28″ long and one rail 1½″ wide × 28″ long.

We don't have to be concerned about industry-standard door sizes with this cabinet, so it can be any width. You can use this cabinet to fill odd-size spaces in many situations. Apply the basic system design rule that inside face frame width should equal inside carcass width, and

Fig. 6-11
This cabinet is almost always installed during a kitchen renovation project.

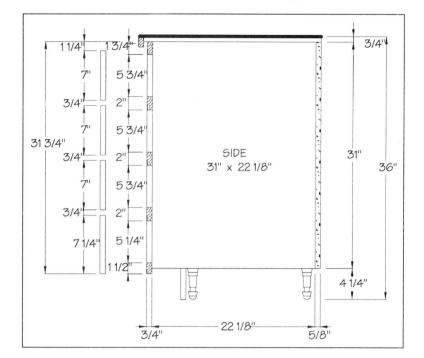

Fig. 6-12
The four-drawer base has some special rail sizes to maintain the 30½" height guideline.

make the cabinet any size you require. For example, if I had to fill a 26⅝" space, I would construct a face frame with 1" wide stiles and rail widths of 24⅝". The carcass bottom board would be 24⅝" wide, equalling the inside face frame width. Remember, you don't have to be concerned with standard door sizes because you can make the drawer faces any width, as long as they are 1" shorter than the outside face frame width. All other carcass boards follow the standard rules: sides are 31" high × 22⅛" wide and the back board width is the total of the base board width and the two side thicknesses by 31" high.

REDUCED-DEPTH BASE CABINETS

You may on occasion require base cabinets that are not as deep as the standard 24" unit. One situation may be where you want a cabinet base run for storage against a wall in a passageway. The easiest solution is to convert the standard

Tip

The only special consideration with sink bases is the issue of particle core board being used where there is a possibility of water damage. Particle core board material and water do not go well together. Also, this cabinet is often used to store liquids for cleaning. For these reasons, I construct the sink base cabinet as a standard 36" base cabinet, using water-resistant plywood painted with a good oil-base paint on the interior of the cabinet.

upper cabinets into base cabinets by attaching adjustable legs. As you may have already noticed, the overall cabinet height and door height are the same for the upper and base cabinets; only the depth is changed. You can purchase or build reduced-depth countertops to accommodate these special base cabinets.

I have, on many occasions, used reduced-depth cabinets in a kitchen island situation. Space is sometimes a problem when designing islands, so I've often reduced the base units to a maximum of 18" deep and installed a 32"-wide

Fig. 6-13

Reduced-depth base cabinets are an ideal solution for an island or snack bar when space is at a premium.

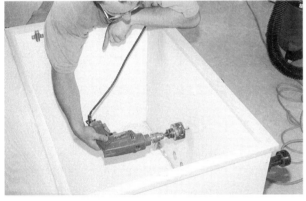

Fig. 6-14

Plumbing and the possibility of water leaks inside this cabinet should be taken into account when designing the sink base.

SINK BASE CABINETS

Sink bases are a standard drawer-over-doors base cabinet, usually a 36″ base, with a false drawer face or drawer face flip-out-over-doors arrangement. The drawer face covers the bottom of the sink when the doors are open.

Install six legs on this cabinet, one at each corner and one at the front and back in the middle of the base, to give it added support. This cabinet usually takes quite a bit of abuse because the supply and drain plumbing pipes must be installed. It's not uncommon to have someone crawling inside the cabinet to install and connect the service. It is also possible that you may have to relocate a cabinet leg if it ends up in the path of a plumbing pipe. You may also have to modify a shelf, if you want one installed, after you determine the location of the pipes inside the cabinet. Leave it until the installation is complete to determine where you will be able to install the shelf. In many cases, shelf installation is not possible because of the plumbing.

island countertop. This allows the countertop to overhang the base cabinets by approximately 13″, taking into account the door width and door side overhang. Stools can be used to provide a casual eating area or as a place to sit while you're preparing food.

CHAPTER SEVEN

Pantry and Microwave Cabinets

Packaging of ready-to-eat foods, including canned goods, dried pastas and prepared foods in bulk, has created a storage problem. The many items on the average family's weekly grocery list that can be stored in the modern kitchen demand an effective, easily accessible storage system. Pantry cabinets designed with adjustable shelving, or the more effective pull-out shelves on drawer glides, are a welcome feature. If you want to maximize storage space, pantry and microwave cabinets are extremely effective.

CONSTRUCTION NOTES

Pantry and microwave cabinets share the same basic carcass assembly. The sides are 80½″ high and as deep as you require, the top and bottom shelves follow the width rules for standard cabinets, and the back is 80½″ high and as wide as the bottom board plus the two side thicknesses. There may also be one or two additional fixed shelves. The face frame is 81¼″ high with 1″-wide stiles and 1½″ top and bottom rails. The face frame may also contain up to five additional rails, depending on the drawer and door combination. Each cabinet is normally fitted with adjustable shelves, drawers, pull-outs or a combination of all three.

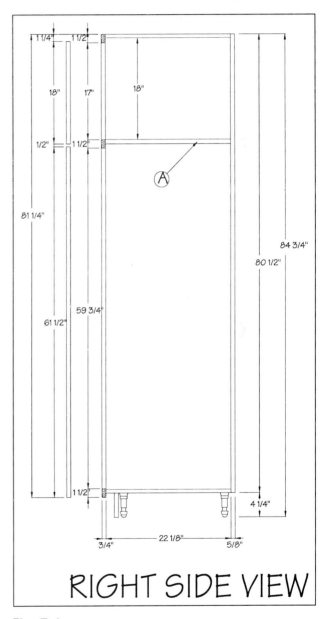

Fig. 7-1

A pantry cabinet is simply an extended high base cabinet.

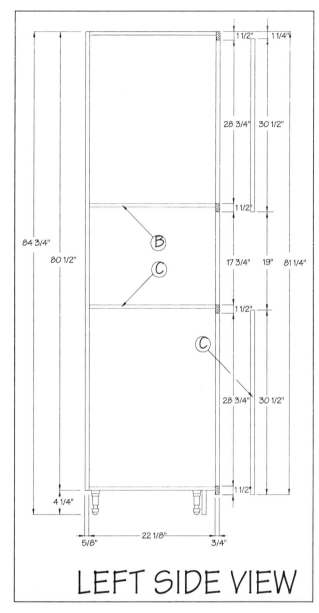

Fig. 7-2

This cabinet is a combination base and upper cabinet with a fixed shelf compartment for the microwave.

LEFT SIDE VIEW

The upper section of the pantry cabinet is high and sometimes very deep. The tendency is to store kitchen utensils that are not often used for day-to-day meal preparation. To better use this space, you might want to consider installing vertical fixed partitions in place of the normal horizontal adjustable shelf. Vertical partitions allow you to store articles such as cutting boards, pizza trays and large serving platters, which usually end up stacked on top of one another in a base cabinet. Simply attach the verticals with two screws through the top of the cabinet and two through the underside of the fixed divided shelf. You don't have to be concerned with shelf loading capacity as these verticals simply define cubicals for large-item storage. Use 5/8″ melamine-coated PCB as the divider partitions, with the plastic edge molding, veneer tape or hardwood edging covering the cut ends.

Figure 7-2 details the construction of a pantry cabinet in which you install adjustable shelves or pull-outs. The pantry cabinet is built using two doors with the lower larger door(s) having three European hinges installed. The

Tip

Individual areas, as well as supplier preferences, determine standards for the supply of veneer-covered particle core board. For example, 11/16″ veneer-covered PCB is a standard in my area. If you can't get 5/8″ veneer PCB, use 11/16″ and adjust your stile width. You can use whatever is commonly available as the cabinet system will easily adapt to any standard.

lower door is an industry-standard 61½″ in height, and the upper door is 18″ high. A ½″ gap is left between the upper and lower doors so that we maintain the 1¼″ space at the top of the face frame. A rail is installed, with a fixed shelf board, at the point where the upper and lower doors meet.

Microwave cabinets, as shown in Figure 7-2, follow all the standard cabinet rules and usually contain a lower drawer bank or pull-outs behind doors, with adjustable shelves behind the upper doors. The middle opening normally contains the microwave. The opening space is large enough for most microwaves using a standard cabinet width of 27″, which has a 25″ inside face frame width. When planning for a microwave cabinet as part of the renovation project, don't forget to have an electrician wire an outlet in the space where the microwave is to be installed.

If you are going to install four drawers in the base of this cabinet, follow the same rules and dimensions that apply to a four-drawer bank base cabinet. Remember to use spacing cleats if you are installing pull-outs behind the doors on either cabinet. The upper sections of these cabinets are normally fitted with adjustable shelves.

The microwave cabinet carcass can be built using wood-veneer-covered particle core board,

as a portion of the cabinet is visible. A ⅝″ wood-veneer board will allow the face frame to extend ⅜″ beyond the carcass, which makes it easy to use the wood doorstop molding around the perimeter that is visible. This technique covers screws and softens the look of these large cabinets.

Microwave and pantry cabinets are simply an upper and a lower with the space between them connected. Install these cabinets before or at the same time as the base cabinets so your maximum cabinet height is defined. This uniformity of height is important for upper cabinet trim installation as well as visual appearance. Since these cabinets are often end-of-run units, finishing trim should be applied, which will be detailed in chapter seventeen.

Don't let the size or apparent complexity of these cabinets bother you. They are simple to build, although somewhat awkward to handle alone. You will probably need someone's assistance during the assembly stage.

The back boards of these cabinets, like all the other standard units, will be installed over the side edges, which reveals the back board edge at the side of the cabinet. These visible edges will be "trimmed out" with doorstop molding after installation to finish the cabinet.

CHAPTER EIGHT

Special Cabinets and Accessories

Almost every kitchen renovation project will require some type of custom cabinetwork. Each project is different, and it's impossible to predict what requirement will arise. However, I believe you'll be able to meet the needs of almost all situations by applying the standard design principles of this cabinet system. The standard upper, base, corner, pantry and microwave cabinets can all be easily modified to meet just about any need.

Fig. 8-1

Apply ¼″ veneer-covered plywood to the exposed end of the cabinet with construction cement and brad nails.

END CABINETS

Base and upper cabinets that are at the end of a run and open to view on one side must be finished so that we don't see the melamine PCB sides. These open end-run cabinets should be identified in the planning stage, prior to cabinet construction.

To allow for the finishing trim that's used on

Tip

On base cabinets I add a ¾″ filler to the bottom of the cabinet side to extend it to 31¾″ so the applied veneer panel will be flush with the bottom of the face frame.

end-run cabinets, increase the stile width by ⅜″ on the side to be finished. Increasing the stile width on standard upper and base cabinets does not alter the dimensions of any other cabinet part. This stile-width-increase technique is needed for end finishing, contour fitting of the cabinet to a wall or custom cabinet fitting of a cabinet run that is closed by walls on both ends. In the planning stage, I normally designate a cabinet that requires increased stile width with a measurement and side designation. A 30″ cabinet that will be used as an open left-end-run cabinet will be shown on my plan as a 30″ plus ⅜″ L upper or base. Standard stile width is 1″, and most wood types, typically oak, pine, cherry and maple. This molding is rounded-over on one side and flat on the other, as shown in Figure 8-2. I install it around the perimeter of the side with the rounded-over side to the inside. It's slightly flexible, so the flat side can contour with any small wall irregularities.

The combined thickness of the veneer plywood and the doorstop molding is greater than $\frac{1}{2}''$, so it's slightly inset on the extended cabinet stile. This type of end-run cabinet finishing looks very professional and adds visual depth to the cabinet side.

The screw holes that secure the end-run cabinet stile to the cabinet rails must be filled with wood plugs so they won't be visible. As stated earlier, I use a $\frac{1}{8}''$ countersink drill bit assembly with a $\frac{3}{8}''$ counterbore hole for these screws. I fill the holes with $\frac{3}{8}''$ wood plugs sanded flush to finish the visible stile sides on these end-run cabinets.

FINISHING UNDER UPPER CABINETS

Some cabinetmakers leave the underside of upper cabinets unfinished. This area, while not normally visible when standing in front of the cabinets, may be seen by someone sitting in the kitchen. It may not be considered a major issue, but I believe finishing this area adds a measure of quality to the cabinetwork.

Install $\frac{1}{4}''$ veneer plywood of the same type as the cabinets, cut to fit, on the underside of the uppers. The front edge of the veneer will not be visible because the face frame extends $\frac{3}{4}''$ below the cabinet carcass. If there is a open end-run cabinet, the end edge of the veneer plywood can be hidden by the doorstop molding that is used to finish the side.

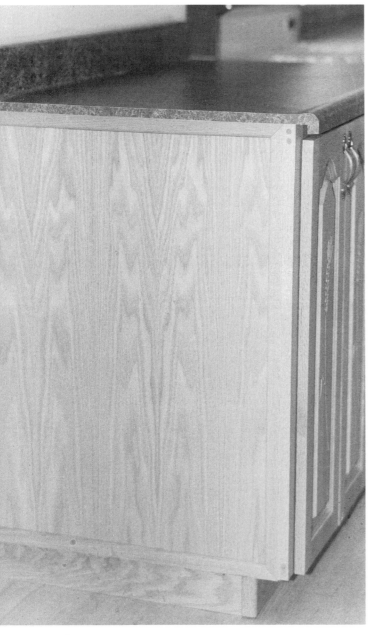

Fig. 8-2

An open end-run cabinet finished with veneer plywood and doorstop molding

standard side thickness is $\frac{5}{8}''$. This means that on a normal cabinet the stile extends beyond the side by $\frac{3}{8}''$. The plus $\frac{3}{8}''$ increase in stile width makes the stile extend a total of $\frac{3}{4}''$ past the side.

After cabinet installation, I install wood doorstop molding around the perimeter of the cabinet end. Doorstop molding is available in

Fig. 8-3
Finishing the underside of the upper cabinets adds a mark of quality to your work.

NONSTANDARD CABINET WIDTHS

There are instances when standard cabinet width is not suitable. Typically, this situation will arise when cabinets are to be installed in a "closed run," such as between two walls in a kitchen. The wall-to-wall distance is often not equal to the combined width of a number of standard cabinets.

The stile width of standard cabinets can be changed without changing any other cabinet component dimension. This procedure was discussed previously under the End Cabinets heading on page 78. The major issue is the visual appearance of the cabinets. If possible, we want to maintain a uniform and balanced look.

A typical situation might be a galley kitchen where the wall-to-wall dimension is 107″. Three 36″ cabinets would be too large because their combined total width is 108″, and any other combination of the standard cabinet widths does not total 107″.

There are two or three solutions to this common problem. The first is to design the cabinet run for that area with one cabinet being a drawer bank. As discussed under the Four-Drawer Base Cabinet heading on page 72, a drawer bank can be any size because it isn't dependent on industry-standard-size doors. The 107″ dimension could be achieved by using two 36″ base units and one 35″ four-drawer bank unit. However, this is not always practical if upper cabinets are to be installed above the base units.

Another option is to increase the stile width of the standard cabinet to achieve the desired total width. A combination of two 36″ cabinets and one 33″ cabinet in the center totals 105″. If the outside stiles (on the 36″ cabinet sides that are against each wall) are both increased by 1″, we will achieve our 107″ wall-to-wall dimension. The extended stiles will look balanced because each cabinet run end will be equal. This can be done with both the upper and lower cabinets against each wall. In situations like this, I add ⅛″ to each wall-side stile so that I can scribe fit or contour the stile to match any irregularities in the walls.

There are other solutions that are possible; however, they are dependent on the location. The closed wall-to-wall run may contain a window so the cabinet combination is very dependent on the size of the window opening. Possibly a sink needs to be installed in that run or you have other specific needs. Many of your solutions will be influenced by your needs, but I believe this cabinet design system is flexible enough to meet those requirements.

Fig. 8-4

Toe kick boards are installed in the adjustable legs with a clip.

TOE KICK BOARD

Toe kick boards are attached to the European cabinet legs with a fastener called a plinth clip. These clips are available from the hardware supplier that provides the cabinet legs. They are attached differently, depending on the manufacturer. One style of clip requires a small dado cut on the backside of the toe kick board and another style is attached with screws in a plastic frame. The boards are easily installed and can be removed when necessary.

There are many advantages to the adjustable leg and removable toe kick board system. They make cabinet installation very simple, and the toe kick boards can easily be removed when the client is installing new flooring material. (Flooring installers like this system because they can remove the toe boards and run the new flooring under the cabinets, thereby avoiding a lot of cut and trim work.) You can remove the toe boards in the event of a water spill and dry the floor under the cabinets, eliminating the possibility of

cabinet damage. When removing old kitchens, I've seen the amount of damage that moisture can cause because cabinet sides and wooden base supports were fastened to the floor. Cabinet legs can prevent this problem. Cabinet life can be extended by installing legs with the removable toe kick board system.

UNDER-CABINET LIGHTING

Under-cabinet lighting is a common accessory in many kitchen renovation projects. There are numerous types and styles of lighting assemblies available, including low voltage and fluorescent fixtures.

I use a fluorescent lamp assembly with this cabinet system mainly because of the energy efficiency of this type of light, as well as its low heat properties. A warm-white fluorescent tube gives an even, soft illumination to the normally dim under-cabinet space.

It's best to decide whether or not you want under-cabinet lighting during the planning stage

Fig. 8-5

Under-cabinet lighting is a real asset in kitchens that do not have natural lighting provided by a window.

because power and switches must be installed. This could be as simple as attaching the power feed line to an existing circuit or bringing in a new line from your service panel. It's best to get all the electrical modifications inspected and approved, based on the codes in your area.

The under-cabinet lighting system consists of a 1″ × 4″ board, of the same type of wood as the doors, mounted on edge under the upper cabinets, approximately 6″ from the wall. Use angle brackets to secure this board under the cabinets. Mount the fluorescent fixture, which is available in 2-, 3- and 4-foot lengths, to the back of the board. I have mounted the fixture to the bottom of the cabinet behind the board; however, the bare bulb can be seen by someone sitting in the kitchen. It's best mounted to the board, making the fixture almost invisible.

CUSTOM CABINETS

There are situations that will arise where your needs can only be met with a custom cabinet. One example would be a requirement to construct a cabinet to fully enclose a fridge. Situations such as this, as well as others you will no doubt be faced with, require that you design and construct very specialized cabinetry.

In the majority of custom cabinetry situations, you can apply the standard cabinet design principles to meet your needs. In the example discussed, you can use a modified version of the 33″ over-the-fridge cabinet. Extend the sides and stiles to meet your overall height requirement, normally 85″, using wood-veneer PCB and hardwood stiles.

Modify how you fasten the top and bottom boards with the use of screws and brackets. If you plan to use wood doorstop as a perimeter trim, place the screws that support the bottom

and top boards in areas where they will be hidden by the trim. Reduce the depth of the top and bottom boards by ⅝″ so the back board is set in flush with the sides in the rear of the cabinet.

Enclosing the refrigerator is a very common situation, so I simply extend the sides and stiles as discussed earlier. The depth of the standard 33″ over-the-fridge cabinet must be increased to fully enclose the fridge. The width of each stile should also be increased to maintain the 33″ inside clearance for the fridge. In most cases, you can use 2″-wide stiles that are notched on the inside to 1″ wide below the bottom rail to the floor. You can also extend the sides and stiles on the 36″-wide standard upper, which gives you a 34″ inside dimension for wide refrigerators.

Custom pantry units are also a popular request. By applying the standard door-to-cabinet-width relationship and the face frame-to-interior-carcass-width principle, I can easily build any size pantry cabinet.

Fig. 8-6

Custom cabinets such as this series designed to enclose a refrigerator are built using the standard cabinets with minor modifications to suit your needs.

CHAPTER NINE
Making Cabinet Doors and Drawers

This kitchen design system is based on buying or building cabinet doors in industry-standard sizes. Manufacturers supply doors in fixed sizes for face frame (traditional North American) and frameless (European) style cabinets. These doors are stock items, mass produced and sold at very reasonable prices. You can order any size door from these suppliers, but once you get away from the standard stock sizes, your costs increase dramatically.

Standard door sizes for face frame (this design) and frameless cabinet styles are described in the following table. All measurements are in inches.

There are one or two restrictions in the combinations of height vs. width, but for the most part all of these combinations are available as a stock item. There are many door suppliers, and some may offer more or fewer combinations of door sizes as standard. You can purchase drawer fronts from these suppliers that match the door style you are using. There are many styles available, so you shouldn't have any trouble selecting a door that suits your taste.

READY-MADE DOORS

You will have to decide whether you want to build or buy your cabinet doors. As a cabinet-making contractor, I find it more economical to buy my doors from a specialty manufacturer. From a business point of view I can't hope to offer all the styles that are readily available from the suppliers. I would have to equip myself with routers, shapers and jigs in many different styles and sizes to be able to offer a competitive selection to my clients.

Many suppliers offer a wide range of styles in all the popular wood species, with four- or

STANDARD DOOR SIZES

Style	Height	Width
Face Frame	10, 13, 16, 18, 21¼, 23½, 28, 30½, 61½	7¼, 8½, 10, 11½, 13, 14½, 16, 17½, 19, 20½, 22
Frameless	15, 18, 24, 30, 32, 49¼	8⅞, 10⅜, 11⅞, 13⅜, 14⅞, 16⅜, 17⅞, 19⅜, 20⅞, 22⅜, 23⅞

five-day delivery schedules. A typical door costing forty dollars from a supplier is made with about fifteen dollars worth of wood. The balance of twenty-five dollars would have to cover my labor if I wanted to offer a product at a competitive price. If the door was a fancy cathedral solid raised-panel style door, I could not cover my labor costs for making it. If the doors were all the same size, the operation might be worthwhile, but this is rarely the case.

BUILDING THE DOOR

Cabinet doors are usually made with 1″ × 3″ stiles and rails. The wood is cut with a router or shaper using a stile-and-rail cutter, which forms the groove for the ¼″ plywood core center or solid raised panel.

Plywood is simply cut to the correct size from a 4′ × 8′ sheet when building center panels for the plycore door. Raised panels are made by gluing up ¾″-thick hardwood and cutting the

Fig. 9-1
A door being assembled using ¼″ veneer-covered plywood for the center panel. This is typically the least expensive frame-and-panel type of door.

edges down to the required thickness with a panel-raising bit. If your rails are to have a design, such as a cathedral top, you have to cut the design in the rail prior to routering. Normally, a door such as a cathedral style has a wider top rail to allow for the curve on the inside edge.

If you're making the kitchen cabinets for yourself, and the cost of your time is not an issue, then building the doors may be a good option. However, you may need to invest in some tools, depending on the style of door that you want to build. Doors such as a solid raised panel with fancy router work can be built. The basic tool will be a good-quality router.

It's possible to produce a very simple and inexpensive door with a ¼″ dado bit. Cut ¾″-thick 1″ × 3″ wood to the required lengths for the stiles and rails, and then dado the inner edges. Assemble three sides, slip in the ¼″ center panel and install the fourth side. If you want something a little fancier, round over the inner and outer edges of the stiles and rails, being careful not to cut into the dado on the inside of the doorframe. When assembling cabinet doors, do not glue the center panel; it has to "float" freely to account for expansion and contraction of the wood.

The slab door is another simple alternative when cost is a factor. Veneer-covered particle core board or plywood, cut to size and edge banded with veneer strips, is an inexpensive option. You can apply ready-made molding designs, which are available at many home centers, to the face of the door.

Tip

To prevent your door panels from rattling, put a little piece of soft foam in the dado before you install the center panels.

Fig. 9-2

Building doors using ¹¹/₁₆″ veneer-covered particle board is an inexpensive and simple option.

Quite often, unique designs can be created with a little imagination. A forty-dollar 4′ × 8′ sheet of veneer-covered particle core board will yield quite a few doors costing under ten dollars per door. I have used slab doors for many applications. The laundry room, bathroom and workshop are just a few of the areas where a very fancy and expensive door is not required. The workshop or basement is where you often need storage cabinets that have doors for dust protection or for securing hazardous chemicals from curious youngsters. Follow all the size specifications for cabinet doors, but replace the more expensive hardwood with less expensive plywood or PCB. You can also use inexpensive furniture-

grade pine for the face frame assemblies. For inexpensive cabinets, I've used ¾″-thick plywood cut into stiles and rails. You can get quite a lot of face frames this way. This gives you an opportunity to practice building and installing cabinets without investing a lot of money.

Solid-core doors are made with a panel-raising router bit plus the rail-and-stile cutter. These combination sets cost in the area of $200. I would suggest that you consider a ½″ collet router when using these bit sets, as they have to do a considerable amount of cutting.

If you're serious about door construction, consider the benefits of having a router table. This piece of equipment, properly aligned, can make raised-panel door construction simpler and will often give you better results than a handheld router. A shaper, although considerably more expensive, is the ideal tool for the production woodworker who wants high-quality results. Shaper bits come in all styles, allowing you to make other items such as fancy custom moldings.

Fig. 9-3

A raised-panel door tends to be the most expensive style because of the solid wood glue-ups required for the center panel.

Door Hinges

The standard hinge used in this system is the 120° European full-overlay door hinge. The two exceptions are the 36″ standard corner base cabinet which uses two 170° full-overlay hinges and two bifold door hinges, and the 170° full-overlay door hinge with a face frame mounting plate for the 24″ standard upper corner cabinet.

Hinge mounting plates are available in many different styles for any of the possible applications that you may encounter. However, this building system uses the standard wing-mounting plate that is attached to the side board in all but one application. The upper corner cabinet side, because of its design, does not line up flush with the inside of the face frame opening. For this reason we use a mounting plate that is designed to be attached to the face frame.

INSTALLING THE HIDDEN HINGE

1 Drill the Door

You will have to drill 35mm flat-bottom holes in the doors with a drill bit specifically designed for hinge installation. Place the hole ⅛″ in from the door edge, which properly orients the doors. There isn't an absolutely correct position for these hinges on the door, but I found installing them at 4″ centers from the top and bottom of the door works very well. Prior to drilling the hinge holes, note the position and side clearances required for pull-outs or other accessories, particularly in the base cabinets.

Invest in the best carbide-type 35mm hinge drill that you can afford. The drill must provide a clean, accurate cut with minimal tear-out around the edge of the hole. Drilling your holes accurately with a good-quality bit will give the hinge a solid mounting position.

2 Mount the Hinge

Mount the hinge on the door in the 35mm hole. Use ⅝″ wood screws. Make sure the hinge wings run parallel to the door edge.

3 Mount the Door

Installing the doors may seem complicated, particularly if you follow suggestions that say you require expensive door-mounting jigs. Fortunately, I've found a way to mount doors correctly and quickly every time without the use of these expensive jigs.

Fig. 9-4

A 35mm hole is drilled on the inside of the door using a Forstner drill bit.

Fig. 9-5

Correct placement of the 35mm hole ensures quick and easy installation of European-style hinges on the door.

Fig. 9-6

Install the mounting plate on the hinge and secure the assembly to the cabinet side with ⅝" wood screws.

Fig. 9-7

The hinge adjusts in three directions, allowing you to accurately place the door in its correct position.

4 | Adjust the Door(s)

Release the mounting plate screws on the hinges and adjust the door so there is a ⅛" gap between the face frame and the door in its open position. Close the door and check its position. Adjust the vertical and horizontal screws, if necessary, to align the door bottom with the face frame bottom and the gap between the doors.

Installing the doors flush with the bottom of the face frame on both upper and lower cabinets is important. This position gives us a 1¼" face frame reveal above the doors which allows for countertop-to-door clearance on the base units and a space to install decorative trim molding above the doors on the upper cabinets.

A door, over the life of the kitchen, may be opened thousands of times, and therefore quality is a real issue. There are a number of hinge manufacturers. Most produce a high-quality product; some, however, supply hinges that are very poor in quality. Grass and Blum are two of the many manufacturers that produce high-quality cabinet hardware, including hinges. I suggest you thoroughly investigate the hardware supplied in your area and choose the best product available. Buying the highest quality hinges will pay dividends in the long run.

Tip

Mount the hinges on the door with the cabinet side board mounting plate attached correctly to the door hinge. Put the door hinges in the open position and place the door in its open position relative to the cabinet, with the bottom of the door flush with the bottom of the face frame. Place screws into the cabinet side through the mounting plate on both hinges. This method will place the door very close to its final position and will require only a slight adjustment.

DRAWERS, PULL-OUTS AND FLIP-OUTS

Kitchen cabinet quality is sometimes judged by the construction style of the drawers. While this is true in some respects, a drawer in a working kitchen does not have to be constructed of solid hardwood with dovetail joints to be high in quality. And drawer construction is not always the absolute measure of craftsmanship.

It is true, however, that a high-quality drawer is a requirement. It should be solid, well-constructed and easy to maintain. Drawers are subjected to a good deal of abuse by normal everyday opening and closing. Spills can occur, grease and grime can build up on the interior and wear on the movable parts is a fact of life.

As discussed earlier, my main goal concerning cabinet drawers was to find a design that was rugged, easily constructed and simple to clean. The last thing I wanted was being called back to repair drawers that were not functioning properly. That wouldn't be good for my business, and my clients would be very annoyed.

The hardware that I wanted to use was the simple and effective European-style bottom-mount drawer glide. It has been in use for many years and, according to many in the industry, is virtually trouble free. As an added bonus, the drawer hardware is very easy to install. After many years of installing these glides, I continue to believe that they are the most reliable drawer system available.

I also wanted to make use of the strips of melamine-coated PCB that were left over from the cutting of cabinet parts. These strips, sometimes as much as seven inches wide, would be ideal for the sides, backs and fronts of the drawer carcass.

DRAWER DESIGN

The final design decision was the construction of a drawer following the same style as the upper cabinet carcass. Joints connecting the sides to the back and front pieces would be simple butt joints, arranged so that the ends of the side boards would be concealed behind the drawer face.

The edges of the drawer carcass can be finished by ironing on melamine tape. Another alternative that I use very often is to cover the edges with ¼″ oak strips that are glued and nailed in place. Use the colored wax stick matching the final cabinet finish. Sand the oak edge smooth and use a round-over bit to slightly ease the corners. Apply the final finish to these strips for a very professional-looking drawer assembly.

Fig. 9-8

Drawers should look good, be easy to maintain and operate efficiently in the cabinet.

BUILDING THE DRAWER

1 ### Assemble the Box
Join the sides to the front and back using 2″ PCB screws in the same manner as the upper cabinet carcass.

2 ### Fasten the Bottom Board
Attach the drawer bottom to the carcass in the same manner.

3 ### Tape the Bottom Board Edges
The bottom board edges are exposed on the sides, so they are covered with melamine veneer tape. The back and front edges of the bottom board do not have to be covered with edge tape because they are hidden.

4 ### Mount the Drawer Face
The drawer face, as previously stated, is solid wood matching the type and finish of the doors. Normally, I use a router and round over or cove the drawer face edge using whichever one more closely matches the door style.

MOUNTING HARDWARE AND DETERMINING DRAWER SIZE

Drawers are mounted in the cabinets using the European bottom-mount drawer glide. In general, most manufacturer's drawer glides require that the drawer's total width be 1″ less than the drawer opening width. For example, if I was putting a drawer in a 24″ base cabinet that has an inside stile-to-stile width of 22″, the total width of the drawer would be 21″. The total height of the drawer should also be 1″ less than the height of the drawer opening for the glides I'm currently using. If the opening height of the drawer

Fig. 9-9
Be sure to drill pilot holes before joining the sides.

Fig. 9-10
Fasten the bottom board using 2″ PCB screws.

Fig. 9-11
Iron-on edge tape is used to cover the exposed edges of the bottom board on each side of the drawer.

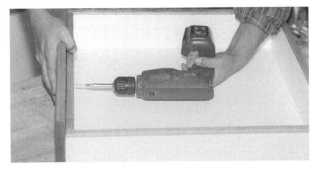

Fig. 9-12
The drawer face is attached with three 1¼″ screws.

space is 6″, the drawer, in total, must be no more than 5″. Drawers for standard bases in this system are 22″ deep on 22″ bottom-mount drawer glides. Given the above, I would need the following pieces to construct the drawer:

- 2 PCB sides @ ⅝″ thick × 4⅛″ high × 22″ long
- 1 PCB back and 1 PCB front @ ⅝″ thick × 4⅛″ high × 19¾″ long
- 1 PCB bottom @ ⅝″ thick by 21″ wide × 22″ long
- 2 solid-wood strips ¼″ thick × ⅝″ wide × 22″ long
- 2 solid-wood strips ¼″ thick × ⅝″ wide × 19¾″ long
- 1 solid-wood drawer face ¾″ thick × 23¹⁄₁₆″ wide × 6¾″ high

The solid-wood drawer face width should equal the width of the door, or total width of the doors plus the gap between the doors when mounted in a drawer-over-door(s) base cabinet. Clearance dimensions are general and dependent on the style of drawer glide used. Refer to the manufacturer's specifications for the brand of drawer glide that you plan to use with your cabinets.

Use two 2″ PCB screws at each corner joint and 2″ PCB screws at 4″ centers on the bottom. The kitchen cabinet hardware supplier in your area should stock small colored plastic screw covers to hide the screw heads on the drawer sides. Remember to use countersunk pilot holes for the PCB screws.

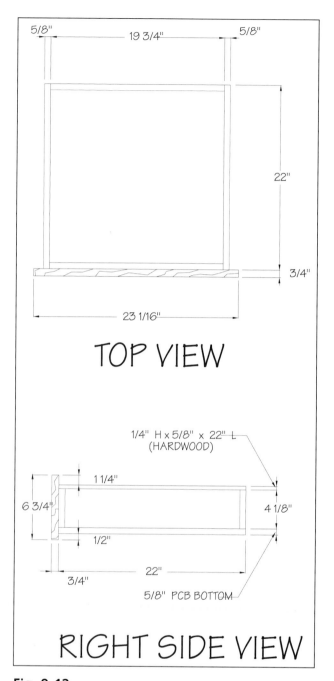

Fig. 9-13

Drawer dimensions for a 24″ base cabinet designed in the drawer-over-door style.

BUILDING PULL-OUTS

Pull-outs in base and pantry-style cabinets have become extremely popular over the past few years. They are a very effective storage option and increase your ease of access when compared to the standard shelf in a base cabinet.

Some styles are directly dependent on client requirements. If a deep pull-out is required, I use the drawer style described previously. It can be as deep as the client requires.

In the last couple of years I have constructed the majority of pull-outs using a ⅝" sheet of melamine-coated PCB mounted on European drawer glides. The front exposed edge of the PCB is covered with plastic cap molding, and the remaining exposed edges have iron-on edge tape applied. A rail system, as shown in Figure

Fig. 9-14
Building a pull-out with commercially purchased plastic rails

9-14, is installed on the PCB pull-out. This is a very effective system for construction, and I recommend it as the standard design.

There is one extremely important design consideration when constructing and installing pull-outs in a cabinet behind doors. The European hinge used in this design has the ability to open in less than the space that it requires for door overlap. In effect, the door mounted with these hinges opens in a space less than ⅝", which puts the edge of the door slightly inside the face frame opening. While this feature is extremely beneficial when two doors are close together, it means that a pull-out will rub or hit the door. To prevent this, 1"×2" cleats are installed on the interior of the carcass, and the drawer glides are mounted to the cleats. The space occupied by these cleats must be taken into consideration when determining your pull-out size.

If you cannot afford to reduce the width of your pull-outs by using the cleat method, you can use 170° opening hinges that clear the interior width of the face frame when fully opened. However, the cabinet door(s) must be opened past the 90° position to clear the space. I tend to use the cleat method with the less expensive 120° hinges in almost all situations.

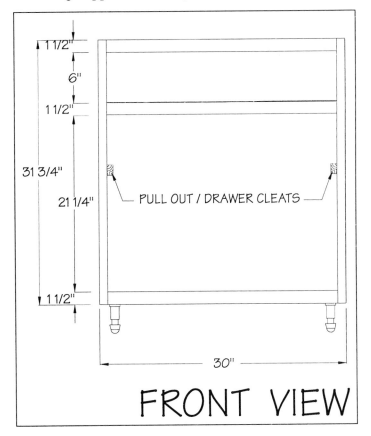

PULL OUT / DRAWER CLEATS

1 1/2"
6"
1 1/2"
31 3/4"
21 1/4"
1 1/2"
30"

FRONT VIEW

Fig. 9-15
A 30" drawer-over-door base is equipped with side board cleats to provide pull-out to door clearance.

BUILDING FLIP-OUTS

Sink cabinets, normally a 36″ standard base, are not usually fitted with 30½″ full-cabinet-height doors. They are built as a drawer-over-door cabinet so that the underside of the sink is not visible when the cabinet doors are open. Obviously the "drawer" is not a functional drawer because the sink occupies the space that is needed for the drawer carcass. The "drawer" is a false face and nonoperational. Until recently this space has been lost.

Various suppliers, such as Rev-A-Shelf Inc., now sell a flip-out kit that comes with hinges and a plastic tray. You can install this kit on the false drawer front and have a functional flip-out drawer face with a plastic tray inside that can be used to store scrubbing pads and dish soap. It's a very popular option and a very easy item to install. Your local kitchen hardware supply outlet should stock these kits.

OTHER DRAWER CONSTRUCTION METHODS AND MATERIALS

If you desire a more traditional-looking drawer or pull-out, hardwoods can be used. Cabinet-grade plywood, sometimes called Baltic Birch plywood, is another alternative that is used quite commonly in the office furniture industry.

Joinery with plywood, and particularly solid wood, can be a little fancier than the simple butt joint. Finger joints can easily be used for drawers made of cabinet-grade plywood, and either finger or dovetail joints can be used with solid wood.

Fig. 9-16
A sink flip-out kit is an inexpensive option and is a useful addition to the sink cabinet.

Fig. 9-17
Hardwood joined by dovetail joints is a very nice touch for the high-end kitchen.

Fig. 9-18
Cabinet-grade plywood, sometimes called Baltic Birch, is an option when you want wood drawers.

CHAPTER TEN

Designing and Building Kitchen Islands

ISLAND DESIGN

Kitchen islands are more popular today as kitchens tend to be built larger. They are a unique and useful design feature in any kitchen. Island workcenters are functional because you have access to the countertop space from all sides. They can be used to define a space, divide a room or add informal seating areas.

In the planning stage, decide whether or not you want the island to be a workcenter or a combination workcenter and seating area. This decision is necessary because you have to alter the depth of the cabinets based on the maximum width of the countertop. If you have 32″ available as your maximum allowable space and you want seating incorporated into the island, you must build your base cabinets 18″ deep. This will leave about 12″ to 14″ of free space for comfortable seating. Remember that an 18″ base cabinet has an additional ¾″ added depth with the doors installed, and you'll need about 1″ overhang on your countertop. Finishing the back of the island base cabinets with veneer plywood and oak trim will add another ½″ in depth. A 32″-wide countertop will leave you with approximately 12″ of free space for stools.

Islands without seating can be standard- or increased-depth base cabinets. However, always

Fig. 10-1

If you have the space, a kitchen island can be a useful and beautiful addition.

calculate the total depth, adding the doors, overhangs and finish trim on the rear of the cabinets. The ends of the island are finished as they are exposed, so remember to account for the extra width when determining your countertop measurements.

Kitchen islands may be true freestanding units or placed against a wall, more properly called a peninsula, and often define traffic patterns in the room. For this reason, countertop edges should be designed and constructed to minimize accidents, particularly with small children.

Fig. 10-2

An island can also have one end attached to a wall to define space and traffic patterns.

Order your island countertops with radius edges, or build the custom countertop style in this book with mitered corners. Always account for the loss in length because of these eased or radius ends when calculating your requirements.

BUILDING THE ISLAND

1 Build the Base

I normally don't use the adjustable legs for island cabinet bases because the cabinets are anchored to the floor. Construct a base platform of 2 × 4s faced with 1″ × 4″ hardwood as the finished kick plate, set back so there is a 3½″ space in from the cabinet edges on all sides. Anchor the cabinets through the base board to the platform.

2 Modify the Face Frame

Build the cabinet with 1⅜″-wide stiles on the face frame, in place of the standard 1″-wide stiles, so you can install veneer plywood and doorstop molding as the finish trim. The back of the cabinet can be finished in the same manner.

3 Change Base Cabinet Depth

Changing the depth of base cabinets for an island workcenter is not a difficult process. The only carcass components that are altered are the depths of the sides and bottom board. All other dimensions remain constant in the standard cabinet. If possible, use the standard-width base cabinets and the changes will be easily accomplished.

In the following example, a 30″-wide standard base is reduced to 18″ deep from the normal 23½″ depth.

As illustrated, the only dimensions changed are the sides and bottom. The same holds true for increased-depth cabinets. These minor changes to meet custom requirements show the flexibility of this building system. You should be able to make minor changes to any of the standard cabinet dimensions to meet all of your needs.

REDUCED-BASE COMPARISON

30″ Base	Standard 23½″ Depth	Reduced 18″ Depth
Two Gables	22⅛″ × 31″	16⅝″ × 31″
One Bottom	22⅛″ × 28¹⁄₁₆″	16⅝″ × 28¹⁄₁₆″
One Back	29½″ × 31″	29½″ × 31″

MOBILE ISLANDS

Kitchen islands that can be moved, sometimes called portable workcenters, also increase the functionality of a kitchen. Additional workspace is often required to meet meal preparation demands. One example is when many people are using the kitchen to help prepare a meal for guests. The ability to arrange temporary work areas helps make the process easier.

Any base cabinet can be adapted for use as a mobile island. For instance, if you want a movable island, construct a standard base unit without the legs. To strengthen the bottom board, at-

tach a piece of ¾″ plywood to the underside of the cabinet. Make certain that the plywood fully covers the bottom of the cabinet. The front edge of the plywood will be hidden by the overhang of the face frame. The sides and back will have ¼″ plywood veneer installed, covering the sides and back edges.

Attach four good-quality wheel assemblies to the bottom of the cabinet. The ⅝″ base board plus the added ¾″ plywood will provide a very solid mounting surface for the wheels.

Buy or build a countertop that overhangs the cabinet on all edges. Angle brackets will secure the countertop to the cabinet. You can also install one of the latest solid-surface countertop materials or even a granite slab.

The interior of the portable island cabinet can be designed in many ways. A standard drawer-over-door base will give you a place to put utensils and other equipment, while a full-door standard cabinet can be fitted with multiple adjustable shelves for cutting boards or equipment storage. Vertical fixed shelving can be used for cutting boards and large trays.

Kitchen islands, whether fixed, peninsula or movable, give you an opportunity to design unique and useful features. They can increase the counter space in a small kitchen and add a bit of flair to a large area. Often, as stated earlier, I use the island and peninsula concepts as area dividers to help define the kitchen space while maintaining the open feeling that most people want in today's kitchens.

Fig. 10-3

Extend the outside stiles by ⅜″ and install wood-veneer plywood to the sides and the back. Trim the perimeter on the sides and back with wood doorstop molding.

Tip

This portable island design is a great addition in your workshop. It can be used as a movable workcenter or tool stand. Build this island with inexpensive ¾″ plywood or particle core board and give it a coat of paint.

CHAPTER ELEVEN
Customizing Your Kitchen

I don't want to get too far off track; however, I thought I'd give you a few ideas for small custom projects for the kitchen that I've come across over the years. The possibilities are endless and the imaginative woodworker will have an outlet to create all kinds of useful accessories for the kitchen.

PROJECT IDEAS
Wine Racks

For the home wine maker, a kitchen wine rack is an excellent accessory. It allows us to display our hard work and have a ready supply of wine for family and friends.

A simple, yet very effective, wine storage and display system can be constructed using the lower half of an upper cabinet. Decide on the space needed for your display and construct a standard upper cabinet with an extra rail. Reduced-height doors are used in place of the standard 30½"-high doors, and the cabinet is constructed from ⅝" wood-veneer-covered PCB.

If you decide to use 18"-high doors, a fixed shelf and rail are positioned so the bottom of the rail is 19¼" from the top edge of the face frame. This will leave an 11" open space in the lower half of the upper cabinet.

A system of wine bottle racks is built using 1"×4" for the front member and 1"×6" solid-wood stock for the rear. Drill 1" holes in the 1"×4" stock and 4" holes in the 1"×6" stock. Po-

sition the holes so that there is approximately ¾" of wood under the holes on each board. Space the holes at 5" centers for the average-sized wine bottles.

Cut the boards at the center line of the row of holes on each board. You'll end up with two front and rear rack members from each board. Cut to the proper width for the cabinet and secure the rack parts in the cabinet with screws through the top. You can use wood plugs to cover the screw holes.

If you want a two-tier rack, install vertical pieces of 1"×2" hardwood behind the front and rear members to support the upper rack assembly. This wine storage system can also be modified by attaching solid-wood sides and using it as a freestanding rack if you have available space on the countertop.

Appliance Garages

An appliance garage is another popular kitchen accessory. It's used for quick access and storage of appliances such as toasters, mixers and food processors. It's best installed under an angled upper corner cabinet.

The tambour is the preferred door style because it is hidden when in the open position and does not occupy any space in front of the garage. Constructing a tambour door and track assembly is time-consuming and fairly complicated, so most of the appliance garage units are purchased as a kit from kitchen supply manufacturers. The kits are reasonably priced and available in most of the popular types of wood. Normally these kits are bare wood that is ready for finishing. They come from the supplier slightly oversized so that you can cut them to custom fit under the cabinet. Follow the instructions with the kit for quick and easy installation. It is a simple little kit but really adds a professional custom look to the kitchen.

Plate Racks

Plate display racks can be added to the space between the upper and lower cabinets. I have installed this accessory in a few kitchens by simply cutting a dado groove in a 1″ × 3″ piece of hardwood and rounding over the edges to soften the look of the rail.

Attach the 1″ × 3″ to the wall by securing with screws driven at an angle, from the underside of the rail, into the wall studs. You can also use small wooden brackets as an alternative method of securing the plate rail assembly.

Above-Cabinet Display

The space above the upper cabinets, typically from ten to twelve inches, is often overlooked as a source of additional storage and display.

You don't have to add any support assemblies to the tops of the upper cabinets, as most display items will sit on the cabinet. In some cases, if the display items are small, a raised platform can be added. However, this space is best used to display pottery, baskets and kitchenware for decorative purposes. I've seen the tops of cabinets used for all types of display, from salt and pepper shaker collections to antique kitchen utensils.

Bookshelves

Today's cooks and hobby chefs have a wealth of information available to them. The average collection of cookbooks and recipe files is large. For those who reference cookbooks often, a bookshelf in the kitchen is a necessity.

Decide on the bookshelf location and dedicate that area to a modified upper cabinet, which you can build using the standard upper cabinet dimensions.

Build a cabinet in the same style as detailed in the upper cabinet section (chapter five) but substitute melamine-coated PCB for wood-veneer-covered PCB. The shelves should be veneer-covered PCB as well. Eliminate the door installation procedures and you have an open upper cabinet assembly with adjustable shelves.

The adjustable shelf system lends itself extremely well to items such as cookbooks. If they are not attractive, you can hide them in a cabinet with adjustable shelves, behind doors.

If you want a small bookshelf, follow the same procedures as detailed for the wine rack storage system. The end result will be a cabinet with reduced-height doors and an open lower-shelf assembly for your cookbooks.

Other Ideas

The possibilities for the woodworker to design and build kitchen accessories are unlimited. I've seen pegboard mounted on 1″ dowels on the inside of doors for storing lids; a spice rack made with ½″ dowels and 1″ × 4″ wood at either end to hold spice bottles in a drawer; and base pullouts to accommodate special needs. Look through magazines and browse the accessories section of the home building supply centers, where you'll find many items that can be built inexpensively in your workshop.

CHAPTER TWELVE
Countertops

At one time, a kitchen countertop was simply a piece of plywood with square edges covered with laminate. I'm sure most of you will remember the imitation "butcher block" design that was so popular in the 1960s. Fortunately, we've realized that countertop material is more than just a covering for the base cabinets. It's understood now that it must be functional, able to stand up to years of use and add design as well as interest to the kitchen.

CONVENTIONAL ROLL TOPS

The simplest and least expensive approach in a renovation project is to use one of the many styles of roll or post-formed laminate countertops that are readily available. Laminate is applied under pressure over a particle core board form that has a curved, molded backsplash and front edge. They are relatively inexpensive and available at countertop specialty companies in most major cities. There are some problems with post-formed tops if a great deal of custom cabinetry is being built, as they are fairly standard in size and design. However, this style can be used in the major portion of most projects.

Post-formed countertops are usually sold by the running foot in three or four widths. You can get bartop countertops, island tops, and pre-assembled or assemble-yourself angled tops. Most countertop suppliers will cut and assemble

Fig. 12-1

Today's countertop materials and styles are numerous. They play an important part in a kitchen and add strongly to the overall design statement.

right-angled countertops, including ones that go from a standard countertop to a bartop on a peninsula. If possible, have the supplier assemble the right-angle runs, as they seem to produce a better joint in their shop than can be achieved on the job site.

Suppliers such as Premoule, Inc. have roll countertop designs called Bull Nose, Flat Top, Tradition, Innovation, etc., and countertop styles such as bartop, regular and island. Finish materials are numerous and varied from manufacturers such as Wilsonart, Formica and Arborite. Costs are reasonable and they can supply countertops for most of your needs.

OTHER COUNTERTOP MATERIALS
Solid-Surface Materials

Another popular material that has recently entered the marketplace is the so-called solid-surface countertop with product names such as DuPont Corian and Wilsonart International Gibraltar. This is an expensive alternative, and installation is normally done by specialists trained by the manufacturers. Not everyone can afford the luxury of this material, but you may find it fits in with your budget. There seems to be an increasing demand and the cost is getting lower as more manufacturers enter the marketplace. Contact local countertop suppliers and speak to them about their pricing schedule, product supply, sample material and literature.

Ceramic Tile

Ceramic tile is used as a countertop material in some kitchen renovation projects. It is one of the oldest and most versatile materials. Available in many sizes, shapes and styles, it's a long-lasting and durable product that lends itself to many design applications. Ceramic tile is resistant to stains and is heat proof. However, the grout lines require constant maintenance due to the

Fig. 12-2
Post-formed roll-top countertops can be used in almost all kitchen renovation projects.

Fig. 12-3
Solid-surface countertop material tends to be expensive but well worth considering.

possibility of staining from food juices. It's best to seal the grout with a high-quality silicone sealer prior to use.

Ceramics are often used on the wall between the upper and lower cabinets because they are easy to clean. Application on the walls is a very straightforward process and fairly simple, as there are normally only three or four rows of tile to apply. Information on wall tile application is available at most tile specialty stores and is quite often a do-it-yourself procedure.

Countertop ceramic tile installation is also a relatively simple operation that requires a bit of skill and a lot of patience. Tile application over water-resistant plywood seems to work well, with the proper glue and grout. Ask the experts at the tile center for the right combination with the product you purchase. Choose the tile and calculate the width of tiles and tile spacing before cutting your plywood to size. With this method you can avoid a lot of unnecessary tile cutting. Band the countertop edge, following tile installation, with a 1″×2″ hardwood strip to match the wood on your cabinets for a professional-looking finish. If you want to avoid a wood edge, you can purchase special edge tiles with a raised lip to complete the installation.

BUILDING CUSTOM WOOD-EDGED COUNTERTOPS

I have seen many, many custom countertop designs and have decided on a style that I use in my business. Basically the design involves using ¾″ high-density particle core board that has been banded with 1″×2″ hardwood of the same type used on the cabinets.

1 Attach the Edge Molding

Fasten the hardwood banding to the edge of the particle core board with 2″ PCB screws and glue. Drill a ⅛″ pilot hole with a ⅜″ countersink bit assembly at 8″ centers. Drill the pilot holes as close to the center of the PCB material as possible.

2 Cover the Screw Holes

Plug the ⅜″ holes with wood plugs and sand smooth.

3 Apply the Laminate

Apply high-pressure laminate to the surface making sure all edges are fully covered, including the top of the 1″×2″ wood edge molding.

4 Trim the Laminate

Trim the laminate with a flush-trim bit in a router.

5 Router the Wood Edge

Use a round-over router bit and cut just to the depth of the laminate. The bottom edge of the wood banding should be rounded over as well, to remove the hard edge and soften the look of the countertop.

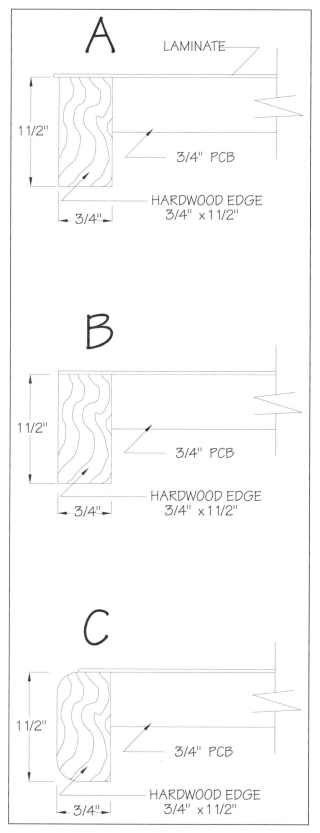

Fig. 12-4

Constructing a custom wood-edged countertop

ANGLED COUNTERTOP CORNERS

If you have children running around or desire a softer look, the corners of the countertop can be angle cut, fitted with the 1"×2" wood banding and sanded round prior to laminate installation and routering.

INSTALLING A BACKSPLASH

Backsplash material is normally 1"×3" hardwood of the same type as the cabinet wood. Attach the backsplash material to the wall with screws in countersunk holes and cover the holes with wooden buttons.

BARTOPS

Bartops are nothing more than wide countertops that are finished on the front and back edges. They can be ordered from any countertop sup-plier or you can make a custom wood-edged countertop. Simply follow the method for the custom countertop style and finish all exposed edges with hardwood. Normally, bartops butt against a wall at one end, so don't finish that end with a wood edge.

ISLAND COUNTERTOPS

Island countertops have four exposed counter edges and are usually a custom width. These top styles can be ordered from the supplier, or you can use the custom wood-edge style.

Bartop, island and peninsula cabinet systems are becoming more and more popular as people tear down walls to create open-concept homes. Base cabinets with fancy tops are created as room dividers, providing workspace but maintaining that open-space feeling. Many of my new kitchen projects use the island and peninsula concepts to add excitement to newly created spaces simply by removing a wall.

Fig. 12-5

Corners on the wood-edged countertop can be angled to soften their look and feel in high-traffic areas or on an island application.

CHAPTER THIRTEEN

Traditional Frame-and-Panel Construction for Cabinets

AN OVERVIEW OF CONSTRUCTION

In earlier times, panel and composites such as plywoods and particle core boards were unavailable. When they began making an appearance, acceptance was limited in the cabinetmaking field. Most cabinetmakers in those days "glued up" solid wood to form a panel for cabinet construction. A number of joints, typically the dado, rabbet and mortise and tenon, are all used in frame-and-panel construction.

Also, the availability of wide solid-wood boards was far greater than today, so it was quite common to have a mill produce full 12″ and larger planks for cabinet work. Most cabinetmakers, like my father, commonly used these wide boards to produce kitchen cabinet parts such as sides and shelves for base units. And solid full-size boards were used to build upper cabinets. Today you would have difficulty locating a solid-wood board over 10″, and if you were lucky enough to find a supply of these boards, they would most likely be very expensive.

As the wider boards began to disappear,

frame-and-panel construction became more popular. This construction style also eliminated the checking and splitting problem common with solid-wood panels. Another beneficial factor that made frame-and-panel construction more acceptable was its reduced-weight properties when compared to a solid-wood panel.

The cabinetmaking system described in this book uses the "look" of traditional frame-and-panel construction when finishing the end of exposed cabinets. Refer to chapter eight, Special Cabinets and Accessories under the End Cabinets heading, page 78.

As the man-made composite boards gained acceptance, frame-and-panel-style construction methods continued to be applied when building cabinets using the new products.

Today's modular-style cabinets were unheard of twenty years ago. Most kitchens were either built as frame-and-panel or "stick" built in place. I often replace older kitchens that were built on the spot, and in most cases the walls play an important part in holding the cabinets in place and together.

Frame-and-panel-style cabinetmaking continues to be a viable option, particularly when building cabinets for turn-of-the-century homes. Dimensions used in this book for man-made composite boards can easily be applied to traditional frame-and-panel construction. A glued-up panel inserted into a hardwood frame is simply one part of a cabinet, much like a PCB cabinet side. The backs, bottoms, tops and shelves of the cabinets are normally solid glued-up wood panels cut to size.

If you're lucky enough to own a turn-of-the-century home and want the look of "original" cabinetry, the frame-and-panel method will give you very dramatic results.

BASE AND UPPER CABINETS

Initially, in the planning stage, make some basic decisions on cabinet style. Do you want absolute authenticity with the turn-of-the-century cabinets or do you want modern features? Adjustable shelves, cabinet legs, removable toe kick boards, pull-outs and modern hinges are interior features that may or may not be a priority.

Base cabinets can have frame-and-panel sides, if they are exposed, and glued-up tops, bottoms and shelves.

Face frames, simply a frame without a panel, are built in the same style as the modern cabinets in this book. However, corner joinery can be mortise-and-tenon, lap joint or dowels to give that old-time look. I would also suggest attaching the face frame to the cabinet face with old-style cut nails, which can be purchased from outlets specializing in antique hardware.

If you want the added feature of adjustable shelves, you can maintain the look of older-style cabinetry by using wood dowel pins in drilled holes in place of the modern plastic shelf supports.

Door hinge choice might cause some difficult-

ies, as older-style hinges do not have the adjustment range or the ability to maintain their position over time. You may have to add a center stile in your cabinet design to allow for hinge movement. The Euro or hidden hinge is very precise and the center stile can be eliminated, but it may defeat the old-time cabinet style appearance that you're trying to achieve. If you want to use antique hinges, add the center stile to the cabinets and install the doors on the cabinet face frame so that you maintain a $\frac{1}{4}''$ gap between doors on two-door cabinets. This will allow you to easily mount the doors, and the door gap will be covered by the center stile. Face frame stile width on the standard cabinet is $1''$, so there should be room to mount the doors, depending on the style of the antique hinges.

You can achieve the traditional frame-and-panel look with your cabinetry and still use all the dimensions in this book. All the cabinet part sizes remain the same, including the doors. If you require a side $22\frac{1}{8}'' \times 31''$, build the frame and panel to that finished size. However, take the thickness of the panel into account when determining cabinet width for shelf, bottom, top and face frame sizes. You may very well have a $\frac{3}{4}''$-thick or greater side. If the standard $30''$ base cabinet requires a $28''$ bottom board, that is referenced to $\frac{5}{8}''$-thick side material. Simply adjust the width of the bottom, top and shelf boards to maintain the maximum standard width to accommodate doors and face frames.

It's also good practice to leave a $\frac{1}{8}''$ space on all sides of the panel in the frame. This allows room for the solid boards to expand should there be high humidity levels in your area. Remember, wood expands and contracts, so to avoid problems, leave room for the panel to float in the frame. Do not glue the panel to the frame (the same rule applies when constructing raised-panel doors).

CHAPTER FOURTEEN
Finishing Cabinets

To completely cover the art and technology of wood finishing in this book would be an impossible task. Fortunately, there are many books devoted entirely to this subject, and the majority are excellent. It would be worth your time to read through some of these publications before choosing the finish for your cabinets.

There are many areas that should be researched when looking for a finishing material, including the most important—safety issues. A good majority of the finishes on the market today are solvent based and can be very harmful if not handled properly. Read the warning labels and pay close attention to products that can cause allergic reactions. If a respirator is called for, wear it. If the manufacturer advises good cross-ventilation, then make sure you finish your cabinets in an area that is well ventilated.

Wood is finished to protect its natural beauty. Many airborne particles, particularly in the kitchen, can stain and discolor wood. Finishing protects and serves to stabilize the fibers as well as reducing the rate of expansion and contraction due to changing humidity levels in the home. A finish adds beauty to the wood, enhances the grain or adds a desired color. It is pleasing as well as protective.

PREPARING FOR FINISHING

Most important, prior to finishing, the wood must be prepared by sanding and cleaning. Sanding removes any of the power tool marks that occur during the planing and dressing stages of cutting lumber. You may also discover dents or gouges in your hardwoods that require repairing. Fill minor abrasions with one of the many wood fillers on the market and prepare the wood as instructed on the container. If the gouge is serious, I'd consider replacing the piece, as it may be more trouble to try to repair the damage. For most filling, such as nail holes and very small gouges, I use a colored wax filler that will match the final finish.

Fig. 14-1

Sanding and preparation are the most important steps to getting a good finish on your cabinets.

Sanding

Begin sanding with a course paper such as 100-grit, move up to 150-grit and finish sanding with 180- or 220-grit paper. I use the 100- and 150-grit papers on a random orbital sander for most of my work, since it will leave very few sanding marks and can be moved in any direction. The final sanding is done by hand with 180-grit paper.

Remember to be very careful with glue on the joints, as it blocks the finish penetrating the wood and can leave a noticeable mark. It's best to wipe the glue with a slightly damp sponge while it's still wet.

TYPES OF FINISHES

There are many finishes available. They include paint and stains in any color imaginable, washed stains, polyurethanes, oils and varnishes. Most finishing products are very easy to apply and produce excellent results. However, check sample finishes on the type of wood you'll be using for your cabinets and research all the properties, both pro and con. Check specifically for the product's hardness, resistance to stains from oils and grease and its life expectancy. The finish will be subjected to a good deal of abuse in the kitchen from heat, moisture and handling.

Fig. 14-2

A few of the many stains, oils and polyurethanes that are available today. Finishing "sample" pieces before you commit to a product is a wise move.

Using Clear, Natural Finishes

About 80 percent of my kitchen cabinets have been finished with a clear satin oil-based polyurethane. The majority of clients seem to prefer the naturally finished wood cabinet. I have also finished a few kitchen projects using the semitransparent washed stains, which are easy to apply and produce excellent results.

Large cabinet shops often use lacquer finishes on their cabinetwork. They apply the lacquer in spray booths with a paint compressor. They produce an excellent finish that dries very quickly, allowing a two- or three-coat application over a very short time period. The spray booth method requires a large space with special ventilation and is beyond the means and space availability of most woodworkers. There are shops that specialize in finishing, and you may want to use their services if one is local.

Wood finishing is an art that takes practice and experience. I have tried many finishes and methods over the years, only to realize that there is much to learn in this field. I have taken finishing courses and read many excellent books on the subject. Good sources of information can be found in woodworking magazines. You will find numerous finishing manuals for sale, as well as many excellent articles on specific finishing techniques in the woodworking magazines.

Applying Polyurethanes

As stated earlier, my preference over the last three years has been to apply the oil-based polyurethane with a good-quality brush. I normally apply three coats, the first coat being thinned, sanding between each coat. The clear satin polyurethane produces a hard finish that doesn't readily show grease or fingerprints and is relatively easy to use.

Over the last two or three years there has

Fig. 14-3

Clear satin polyurethane is a popular choice when finishing kitchen cabinets.

been a move towards the safer, more environmentally friendly water-based finishes. Latex polyurethane is one of these newer finishes that is water based, quick drying and gives off very little odor. However, I find that some water-based finishes tend to raise the grain, as water will do on wood, and produce a slightly cloudy finish. Other cabinetmakers I have spoken with use nothing but water-based finishes, which shows that the use of different finishing techniques and materials is a personal choice.

Finishing is critical to the final product, particularly with wood cabinets. I would suggest that you start with the oil- or water-based polyurethanes and learn as much as possible about other products on the market. Document the finish used in each project file because you may have to duplicate the results when building additional cabinets.

The best advice I can give is to test three or four finishes on samples of the wood you want to use. Evaluate the results by viewing the test pieces in the room where the cabinets will be installed. It's worth the extra effort, as it's difficult to change an applied finish once the project has been completed.

CHAPTER FIFTEEN
Creating Material Lists and Cutting Plans

THE FLOOR PLAN

A floor plan of the kitchen you are about to build is an important first step. It is your information source and road map to completing the project successfully. Draw the plan to scale so that any potential problems can be discovered before beginning construction. You'll find this exercise is valuable and well worth your effort.

There are design software programs, costing between $50 to $100, on the market. Some allow you to render a 3D image of the proposed kitchen on the screen. A few programs allow you to "move" around in the kitchen, showing different perspectives of the cabinets.

However, the most important exercise is drawing a simple scaled overhead floor plan, as illustrated in Figure 15-1. Accurately measure the room dimensions, locating all the doors, windows and any special features of the walls. You may have a plumbing run or heating duct pipe that has been boxed in with drywall that creates a "bump out" on the wall. These special features have to be accounted for, as they may change your cabinet installation procedures.

Using graph paper, scale the cabinets on your plan to get an accurate representation of the size and location of each unit. Check the work triangle distances and traffic patterns, and the direction of opening with the cabinets, refrigerator and microwave.

The ideal floor plan is difficult to achieve given the dimensions of many kitchens. For example, the floor plan in Figure 15-1 places the refrigerator at one end of the room and the sink on another wall at the other end of the room. The distance is greater than it should be for comfortable food preparation, but because of power requirements and the location of other appliances, we were forced to compromise. A table placed in the center of the room will seriously affect the traffic pattern. So, in this case, a kitchen table was placed against the wall opposite the stove/fridge wall. It was the best alternative to many possible floor plans that were analyzed.

This floor plan is shown to illustrate a point, that you sometimes have to work in existing rooms that do not allow you to follow all the accepted "normal" design practices. It's not an uncommon situation, and I'm sure some of you will be faced with design challenges such as this.

One alternative would be a complete relocation of existing services. However, this project, because it was a kitchen in an old three-level apartment building and because of budget constraints and tenants, did not allow changes to existing services.

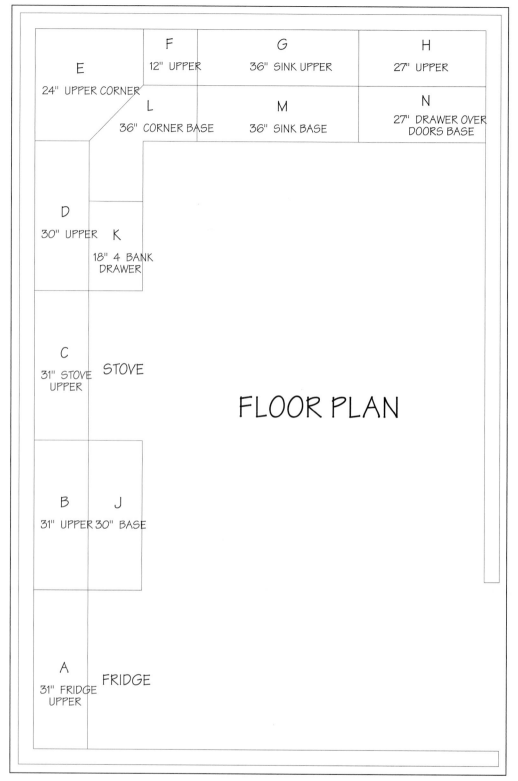

Fig. 15-1

A simple floor plan is needed before any cutting is done. This step should be done at the initial design stage. You may find that three or four plans are required before you get the final design.

⅝″ WHITE MELAMINE PARTICLE CORE BOARD CUT LIST

Cabinet Style and Identifier	Cut Size Required	Cut Size Ref. Number
A - 33″ FRIDGE UPPER (17¼″-High Face Frame) Plus ½″ Left	2 Sides @ 10⅝″ × 16½″	1, 2
	1 Bottom @ 10⅝″ × 31¹⁄₁₆″	3
	1 Top @ 10⅝″ × 31¹⁄₁₆″	4
	1 Back @ 32½″ × 16½″	5
	1 Shelf @ 10⅝″ × 31″	6
B - 30″ Standard Upper	2 Sides @ 10⅝″ × 31″	7, 8
	1 Bottom @ 10⅝″ × 28¹⁄₁₆″	9
	1 Top @ 10⅝″ × 28¹⁄₁₆″	10
	1 Back @ 29½″ × 31″	11
	2 Shelves @ 10⅝″ × 28″	12, 13
C - 31″ Stove Upper (19¼″-High Face Frame)	2 Sides @ 10⅝″ × 18½″	14, 15
	1 Bottom @ 10⅝″ × 28¹⁄₁₆″	16
	1 Top @ 10⅝″ × 28¹⁄₁₆″	17
	1 Back @ 29¹⁄₁₂″ × 31″	18
	1 Shelf @ 10⅝″ × 28″	19
D - 30″ Standard Upper	2 Sides @ 10⅝″ × 31″	20, 21
	1 Bottom @ 10⅝″ × 28¹⁄₁₆″	22
	1 Top @ 10⅝″ × 28¹⁄₁₆″	23
	1 Back @ 29½″ × 31″	24
	2 Shelves @ 10⅝″ × 28″	25, 26
E - 24″ Corner Standard Upper	2 Sides @ 10⅝″ × 31″	27, 28
	1 Bottom @ 22⅛″ × 22⅛″	29
	1 Top @ 22⅛″ × 22⅛″	30
	1 Back @ 22¾″ × 31″	31
	1 Back @ 22⅜″ × 31″	32
F - 12″ Standard Upper	2 Sides @ 10⅝″ × 31″	33, 34
	1 Bottom @ 10⅝″ × 10¹⁄₁₆″	35
	1 Top @ 10⅝″ × 10¹⁄₁₆″	36
	1 Back @ 11½″ × 31″	37
	2 Shelves @ 10⅝″ × 10″	38, 39
G - 36″ Over-The-Sink Upper	2 Sides @ 10⅝″ × 18½″	40, 41
	1 Bottom @ 10⅝″ × 34¹⁄₁₆″	42
	1 Top @ 10⅝″ × 34¹⁄₁₆″	43
	1 Back @ 35½″ × 18½″	44
	2 Shelves @ 10⅝ × 34″	45, 46

⅝″ WHITE MELAMINE PARTICLE CORE BOARD CUT LIST
(Continued From Previous Page)

Cabinet Style and Identifier	Cut Size Required	Cut Size Ref. Number
H - 27″ Standard Upper	2 Sides @ 10⅝″ × 31″	47, 48
	1 Bottom @ 10⅝″ × 25¹⁄₁₆″	49
	1 Top @ 10⅝″ × 25¹⁄₁₆″	50
	1 Back @ 26½″ × 31″	51
	2 Shelves @ 10⅝″ × 25″	52, 53
J - 30″ Standard Base	2 Sides @ 22⅛″ × 31″	54, 55
	1 Bottom @ 22⅛″ × 28¹⁄₁₆″	56
	1 Back @ 29½″ × 31″	57
	1 Shelf @ 22⅛″ × 28″	58
K - 18″ Four-Drawer Bank Base	2 Sides @ 22⅛″ × 31″	59, 60
	1 Bottom @ 22⅛″ × 16¹⁄₁₆″	61
	1 Back @ 17½″ × 31″	62
	8 Drawer Sides @ 3⅜″ × 22″	63, 64, 65, 66, 67, 68, 69, 70
	8 Drawer Backs & Fronts @ 3⅜″ × 13¾″	71, 72, 73, 74, 75, 76, 77, 78
	4 Drawer Bottoms @ 15″ × 22″	79, 80, 81, 82
L - 36″ Corner Base Unit	2 Sides @ 22⅛″ × 31″	83, 84
	2 Sides @ 22⅝″ × 31″	85, 86
	1 Back @ 18″ × 31″	87
	1 Bottom @ 33⅜″ × 33⅜″	88
N - 27″ Standard Base With Drawer Over Doors	2 Sides @ 22⅛″ × 31″	89, 90
	1 Bottom @ 22⅛″ × 25¹⁄₁₆″	91
	1 Back @ 26½″ × 31″	92
	1 Shelf @ 22⅛″ × 25″	93
	2 Drawer Sides @ 4⅛″ × 22″	94, 95
	2 Drawer Back & Front @ 4⅛″ × 22¼″	96, 97
	1 Drawer Bottom @ 22″ × 24″	98

¾″ PLYWOOD CUT LIST

Cabinet Style and Identifier	Cut Size Required	Cut Size Ref. Number
M - 36″ Standard Base (Plywood Sink Base)	2 Sides @ 22⅛″ × 31″	99, 100
	1 Bottom @ 22⅛″ × 34¹⁄₁₆″	101
	1 Back @ 35⁹⁄₁₆″ × 31″	102

¾″-THICK WOOD FACE FRAME CUT LIST

Cabinet Style and Identifier	Cut Size Required	Cut Size Ref. Number
A - 33″ Fridge Upper (17¼″-High Face Frame) Plus ½″ Left	1 Stile Left @ 1½″ × 17¼″ 1 Stile Right @ 1″ × 17¼″ 2 Rails @ 1½″ × 31″	1 2 3, 4
B - 30″ Standard Upper	1 Stile @ 1″ × 31¾″ 1 Stile @ 1½″ × 31¾″ 2 Rails @ 1½″ × 28″	5 6 7, 8
C - 31″ Stove Upper (19¼″ Face Frame)	2 Stiles @ 1″ × 19¼″ 2 Rails @ 1½″ × 28″	9, 10 11, 12
D - 30″ Standard Upper	1 Stile @ 1″ × 31¾″ 1 Stile @ 1½″ × 31¾″ 2 Rails @ 1½″ × 28″	13 14 15, 16
E - 24″ Corner Standard Upper	4 Stiles @ ¾″ Angled at 22½° × 31¾″ 2 Rails @ 1½″ × 13⁹⁄₁₆″	17, 18, 19, 20 21, 22
F - 12″ Standard Upper	2 Stiles @ 1″ × 31¾″ 2 Rails 1½″ × 10″	23, 24 25, 26
G - 36″ Over-the-Sink Upper	2 Stiles @ 1″ × 19¼″ 2 Rails @ 1½″ × 34″	27, 28 29, 30
H - 27″ Standard Upper	2 Stiles @ 1″ × 31¾″ 2 Rails @ 1½″ × 25″	31, 32 33, 34
J - 30″ Standard Base	1 Stile @ 1″ × 31¾″ 1 Stile @ 1½″ × 31¾″ 2 Rails @ 1½″ × 28″	35 36 37, 38
K - 18″ Four-Drawer Bank Base	1 Stile @ 1″ × 31¾″ 1 Stile @ 1½″ × 31¾″ 1 Rail @ 1½″ × 16″ 1 Rail @ 1¾″ × 16″ 3 Rails @ 2″ × 16″	39 40 41 42 43, 44, 45
L - 36″ Corner Base Unit	2 Stiles @ 2″ × 31¾″ 2 Rails @ 1½″ × 11¼″ 2 Rails @ 1½″ × 10½″	46, 47 48, 49 50, 51
M - 36″ Standard Base (Plywood Sink Base)	2 Stiles @ 1″ × 31¾″ 3 Rails @ 1½″ × 34″	52, 53 54, 55, 56
N - 27″ Standard Base With Drawer Over Doors	2 Stiles @ 1″ × 31¾″ 3 Rails @ 1½″ × 25″	57, 58 59, 60, 61

CABINET DOOR LIST

Cabinet Style and Identifier	Door Size	Quantity
A - 33″ Fridge Upper (17¼″-High Face Frame) Plus ½″ Left	16″ Wide × 16″ High	2
B - 30″ Standard Upper	14½″ Wide × 30½″ High	2
C - 31″ Stove Upper (19¼″ Face Frame)	14½″ Wide × 18″ High	2
D - 30″ Standard Upper	14½″ Wide × 30½″ High	2
E - 24″ Corner Standard Upper	14½″ Wide × 30½″ High	1
F - 12″ Standard Upper	11½″ Wide × 30½″ High	1
G - 36″ Over-the-Sink Upper	17½″ Wide × 18″ High	2
H - 27″ Standard Upper	13″ Wide × 30½″ High	2
J - 30″ Standard Base	14½″ Wide × 30½″ High	2
K - 18″ Four-Drawer Bank Base	17″ Wide × 7″ High Drawer Face 17″ Wide × 7¼″ High Drawer Face	3 1
L - 36″ Corner Base Unit	10″ Wide × 30½″ High	2
M - 36″ Standard Base (Plywood Sink Base)	35⅛″ Wide × 6¾″ High False Drawer Face 17½″ Wide × 23½″ High	1 2
N - 27″ Standard Base with Drawer Over Doors	26⅛″ Wide × 6¾″ High Drawer Face 13″ Wide × 30½″ High	1 2

CREATING A MATERIALS LIST

Once the floor plan is finalized, a materials cut list should be created. This list will allow you to calculate how much material to order and provide you with a system to number each finished piece. An average kitchen requires one hundred or more PCB pieces, so this list is invaluable during the assembly phase of your project.

The previous tables detail the ⅝″ white melamine particle core board material cut sizes that are required for the kitchen in the floor plan.

Tip

I set my table saw to 10⅝″ and make all the rip cuts at that dimension. I then set the saw for the next rip cut size. This method eliminates the need to constantly change the saw and gives uniformity to cuts of the same dimension. It is difficult to set the saw at exactly the precise dimension each time. By setting it once for the rip cuts at 10⅝″, I'm sure that all the pieces are the same dimension.

Preparing the cut lists should take you one to two hours, depending on the complexity of the kitchen design. However, it will probably be the most effective two hours that you'll spend building the kitchen. These lists are critical, as they define the sizes of the finished pieces for the carcasses, face frames, doors and drawer faces.

I transfer the carcass cut list sizes to a diagram of 4′ × 8′ sheet material. Sheets are drawn with the reference numbers relating to each individual piece. Once completed, this layout provides information on the number of pieces of 4′ × 8′ material you will require. This process also minimizes waste because you can move pieces around to get the best results prior to cutting. The quantity of sheet goods required is also necessary when calculating your material cost.

Preparing the cut lists and sheet layout diagrams reduces the amount of time required to cut the cabinet parts to size. Cutting the 4′ × 8′ material can be a tiring and time-consuming process without proper planning.

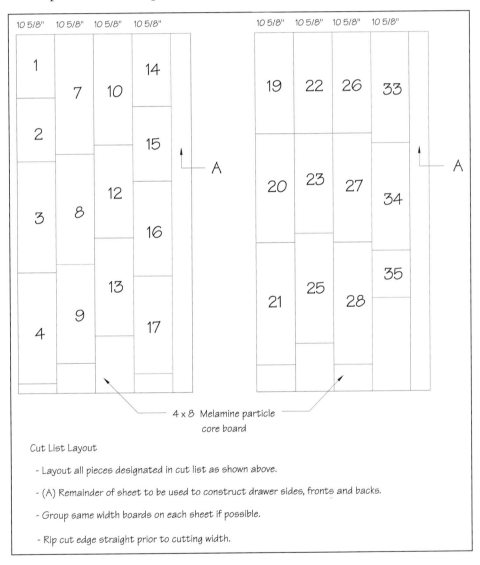

Fig. 15-2

Lay out all the required cabinet boards in boxes that represent the 4′ × 8′ sheets of wood.

CREATING A HARDWARE LIST

The hardware requirements should also be calculated during this planning and layout phase. It doesn't have to be precise to the last screw required, but it should be a fairly accurate representation of the hardware needed. Material ordering and cost can be calculated based on this list. The following is a typical hardware list, based on the design.

COUNTERTOP REQUIREMENTS

The countertop size should be calculated at this time. For our sample kitchen we will need a 30¾″ run for cabinet J. We want ⅜″ overhang on each side. Both sides should have a ¼″ veneer panel (no molding is needed) beside the stove and fridge. The other countertop section required will be a right-angle joined section. The left-side run will be 54⅜″ long (this dimension

HARDWARE REQUIREMENTS LIST

Item Description	Quantity
2″ Particle Board Screws	500
⅝″ Hinge and Angle Clip Screws	200
Cabinet Legs	30
Plinth Clips for Toe Kick Boards	12
Countertop Angle Brackets	25
2″ Spiral Finishing Nails	100
Adjustable Shelf Pins	60
100° Full-Overlay Hinge Assembly	38
170° Full-Overlay Hinge Assembly	4
Double-Door Hinge Assembly for Corner Base Cabinet	2
18″ Full-Round Lazy Susan	1
32″ Pie-Cut Lazy Susan	1
Door and Drawer Handles	27
Door Bumpers	50
22″ European Drawer Glides	5
Cut-to-Fit Cutlery Tray for Cabinet K	1
⅝″ Plastic Cap Molding for Shelves	40 Feet
Door-Mounted Towel Rack for Base M	1

includes the ⅜" overhang on the left side of cabinet K), and the right leg will be 99" long with an unfinished end.

If the countertop is custom fabricated, as detailed under Countertops in chapter twelve, you will have to order the PCB, 1"×2" hardwood edge, 1"×3" wood for the backsplash, and laminate. If it's to be a standard unit from a local supplier, send your order in, as there can be a delay if the design that was chosen is not locally stocked. This issue of stock countertop designs should be discussed with your supplier to avoid delays, as some designs can take four to six weeks to arrive from the manufacturer.

ADDITIONAL MATERIAL REQUIREMENTS

Material required for finishing should also be calculated at this stage, including:

- ¼" veneer-covered plywood for finishing the exposed sides of cabinet J, the left side of cabinet K and half the exposed sides of cabinets B, D, F and H. This veneer plywood is also required to cover the underside of the upper cabinets.
- 1"×4" hardwood for the toe boards
- top molding for the upper cabinets

Tip

For the countertop ends on each side of the stove, order a "profile" edge instead of a "full-finished" edge. The profile style is not built up with a filler piece, so it won't bind against the cabinets if your cabinet run is slightly longer because of wall irregularities.

CREATING A PROJECT FILE

I create a working file for the project. I include my notes on the various designs and changes, the approved layout, my cut lists, order lists and any other information relating to the project. As the project proceeds, I will add information on ordering, the hardware style numbers and final comments after the project is completed.

I find the file system to be one of my most valuable tools. I can refer to the project at any time and use the information if similar projects arise in the future. Also, you may run into a situation where you need an extra door handle or replacement door, or you may want to add another section two or three years down the road.

Project Planning

I lay out all my needs on the cut lists, order the materials, get firm delivery commitments from any sub-contractors such as my countertop supplier or cabinet door supplier, and calculate shop time needed to build the cabinets. I can then realistically plan when to tear out the old cabinets and install the new kitchen. This gives you the opportunity to arrange for the other required services such as new flooring installation, new appliance delivery, the plumber or possibly an electrician.

The planning stage is very critical: A project can turn into a real nightmare if you make mistakes at this point in the process. I'm not suggesting that this is a difficult process—it's actually very simple. Unfortunately, many people do not pay enough attention to this process and get into serious trouble. Analyze all the required steps, detail your material needs, estimate realistic time frames based on the data and keep the other people who you will have to depend on informed about your progress.

CHAPTER SIXTEEN
Shop Assembly Procedures

Following the completion of the cut lists and the purchase of the material, I begin the assembly process in the shop.

1 **Build the Face Frame**
Cut to size and assemble the hardwood face frames so they can be sanded and finished. For this particular kitchen project, I finished the face frames with three coats of clear satin polyurethane. Do not finish the backside of the face frame, as it will be glued to the carcass edge.

2 **Assemble the Door**
Doors can be assembled and finished with the face frames while the carcass cutting and assembly is taking place.

3 **Cut the Carcass Parts to Size**
Rip the 4' × 8' sheets of white PCB and plywood for the sink base to size with the aid of the cut lists and layout sheets. Melamine-coated particle core board edges chip very easily, so special precautions must be taken. Primarily, your table saw should be equipped with a carbide-tipped triple-chip PCB blade. Even though this blade greatly reduces the edge-chipping problem, there is some edge damage to the melamine coating. The tendency, particularly with my saw and many others that I have used, is to chip on one side more than the other. I orient the boards during cutting so the "good side" is always maintained. The only boards that will be exposed on

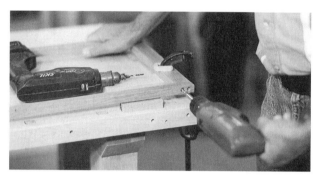

Fig. 16-1
One method of face frame assembly is accomplished by using the butt joint with glue and 2" screws.

Fig. 16-2
Now, build and assemble the doors of your choice.

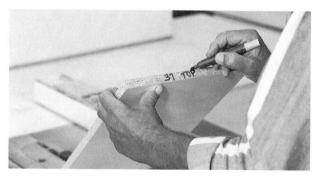

Fig. 16-3
Cut the 4' × 8' sheets of PCB into finished sizes and mark each piece with its reference number.

both sides are the shelf boards and the drawer carcass sides. Chipping can be minimized on these boards by double cutting (the saw blade is set at half the thickness of the melamine PCB, cut on one side and then flipped over to complete the cut). Mark each ripped board, noting the reference number on each piece.

4 Crosscut the Ripped Boards

Following the ripping process, crosscut the boards on a radial arm saw. If the boards are extra wide, as in the case of the base cabinet boards, I use a sliding table attachment on my table saw, or you can just as easily use a circular saw and straightedge. Since the saw chips on one side more than the other, orient the boards paying attention to the board's "good side." Mark each piece with its reference number.

5 Drill Adjustable Shelf Holes

After verifying the board sizes, begin the assembly of the cabinets. Upper cabinet sides are first drilled for the adjustable shelf pins.

6 Assemble the Upper Cabinet Carcass Parts

Following the drilling, fasten the sides to the top and bottom boards with 2″ particle core board screws. The back is installed flush with the bottom and top boards as well as one side board. When using the 2″ PCB screws, make certain that a ⅛″ pilot hole is drilled through the board to be secured and into the center of the edge of the second board. Use a marking gauge set at 5⁄16″ as a guide for the drill bit. The screws should be tight; however, be careful they are not overtightened, which may cause the threads made by the screw in the pilot hole to strip. I use a ⅛″ drill bit in a carbide-tipped ⅜″ countersink assembly to a depth that allows the screw head to be set flush with the surface of the PCB.

Fig. 16-4
Ripped boards can also be cut on the radial arm saw.

Fig. 16-5
Drill the holes for adjustable shelving in all upper and base sides as required.

Fig. 16-6
Assemble the upper cabinet carcasses.

7 Trim the Back Board

Since the backs are cut wide, as previously described, trim the excess flush with the side after fastening the back on all four edges. A square-cut back board will ensure that the cabinet is square.

8 Install the Upper Cabinet Face Frames

Install face frame on the cabinet, making sure of the orientation of any "special" face frames. For example, cabinet A has an 1½" stile on the left side, designated on Figure 16-8 as +½" L, so the face frame must be installed with respect to that orientation. The face frame outside top is set flush with the carcass outside top. The carcass edges should be hidden; then the face frame is glued and nailed to the carcass as previously described.

9 Install Cap Molding

Cut the plastic cap molding to fit the exposed edge of the shelves and secure with contact cement or a glue gun. The cap molding fits very tightly on the ⅝" melamine; however, I add a little glue to make sure it's held firmly in place.

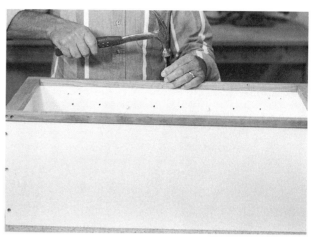

Fig. 16-8
Install the face frame with glue and 2" spiral nails.

Fig. 16-9
Cap molding is installed on the front edge of the shelf.

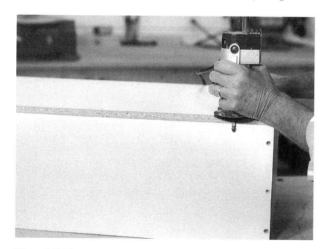

Fig. 16-7
After installing the back board, trim it flush with a router.

Fig. 16-10
Before base cabinets are assembled, make sure to note any special features of each cabinet.

10 Assemble Base Cabinet Parts

The first step in assembling the base cabinets is determining whether or not the cabinet will have a shelf or pull-out installed. Drill holes for the shelf pins or fasten the wood cleats at the correct height, with 1¼″ screws in pilot holes through the outside of the cabinet side into the cleat.

11 Install Cabinet Legs

Install the cabinet legs, four on cabinets under 30″ and six on cabinets over 30″, on the base bottom board. Legs are installed so that they extend out from the base board by ⅝″ to help support the sides. The exception is when the cabinet is open-ended and the toe kick board has to be recessed 3½″ from the cabinet edge, as in the case of base cabinets J and the left side of K. Install the cabinet legs so that they are 3½″ back from the face edge of the base board. Do not fully tighten the leg assemblies at this time, as they may not allow the bottom edge of the side to be flush with the bottom of the base board. They can be tightened after the cabinet carcass is fully assembled.

12 Join Cabinet Parts

Fasten the sides to the base board and install the back board. When installing the back board, verify that the inside dimension of the cabinet is correct at the top of the cabinet, between the two sides. The base cabinet does not require a top board; however, you must make sure the inside dimension, at the top, is correct to guarantee a square and plumb cabinet.

13 Install Countertop Brackets

Install the countertop brackets with ⅝″ screws.

Fig. 16-11
Cabinet legs are installed so that we have the required 3½″ setback on the front for the toe kick space.

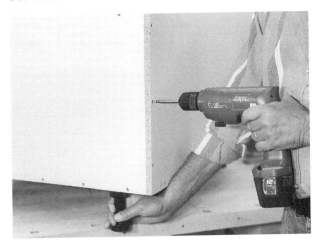

Fig. 16-12
Base cabinets can now be assembled.

Fig. 16-13
Install the countertop brackets.

14 Install the Face Frame

Install the face frame as previously described, noting any special orientation. Check that the top of the face frame is flush with the top of the sides and the side overlaps are equal.

15 Apply the Side Veneer

At this point, cut to size and apply ¼" plywood veneer to any cabinet side that will be visible. In the sample layout, veneer plywood will be contact-cemented to the right and left sides of cabinet J, the left side of cabinet K, the right and left sides of cabinet B, the left side of cabinet D, the right side of cabinet F and the left side of cabinet H. On the upper cabinets, extend the veneer plywood below the side so that it will cover the end of the veneer plywood that will be applied to the underside of the upper cabinets. If you want to add wood doorstop molding as a perimeter trim with standard 1"-wide stiles, you must use a thinner veneer. Apply a ⅛"-thick, or less, veneer to the cabinet sides so that you can use the ¼"-thick wood doorstop molding.

16 Assemble and Install Drawers

Assemble the drawers, as previously detailed in chapter nine, page 89, and check the operation. Follow the drawer glide manufacturer's instructions with respect to clearances. Drawer side clearances are very critical. Try to be as accurate as possible with your cutting and assembly procedures.

Fig. 16-15

Apply ¼" veneer panels to any cabinet sides that will be exposed.

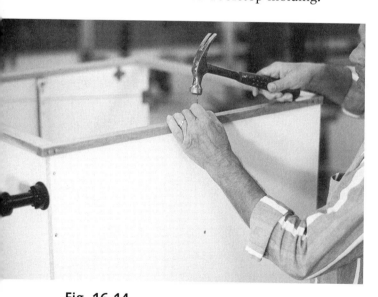

Fig. 16-14

Carefully line up the face frame on the cabinet and attach it with nails and glue. Biscuit joints are another joinery option if you want to avoid filling the nail holes.

Fig. 16-16

Assemble the drawers and install the drawer glides to the drawer and cabinet sides.

17 Install the Doors

Drill the doors with a 35mm flat-bottom drill bit at 4″ centers from the top and bottom of the door and ⅛″ in from the door edge. Pay particular attention to the door orientation if the door is designed with a top and bottom. Some door styles can be reversed, while other designs, such as a cathedral style, must be installed one way. In some instances you have a right and left door and, with single-door cabinets, the side you want the door to open will determine where the holes are drilled. Mount the doors on the cabinets as previously described in chapter nine, pages 86-87.

18 Attach Handles

Make sure the holes are properly spaced for the handles being used, and plumb or level the door edge or drawer front edge.

19 Dado the Toe Kick Board

Make sure the holes are properly spaced for the handles being used, and plumb or level the door edge or drawer front edge. Cut a groove on the back of the toe kick board to ac-

cept the plinth clip assembly. Leave the toe kick boards longer than required to allow custom fitting during installation.

This completes the assembly process and the cabinets are ready to be installed. Compare the cabinets with the layout, noting any special features such as drawers, pull-outs, wider stiles, and door opening direction, to guarantee that all dimensions and requirements are correct.

Fig. 16-18

Install the handles on the cabinet doors.

Fig. 16-17

Drill the doors, install the hinges and attach them to the cabinet sides.

Fig. 16-19

A small dado, usually the thickness of a saw blade, is cut into the back of the toe kick board. Other leg clip assemblies are attached with screws.

CHAPTER SEVENTEEN
Cabinet Installation

EXISTING CABINET TEAR-OUT

Unless you're building cabinets for a new home, you'll be faced with tearing out the existing kitchen cabinets. And unless they are reasonably modern cabinets, you'll most likely find that they were built in place.

Carpenter or stick-built in place cabinets depend heavily on the structural support from existing walls. Therefore, finding fastening devices such as screws and nails can sometimes be quite a challenge. I've seen every fastening device under the sun when tearing out existing cabinets. It can sometimes be very funny to see some of the support systems that have been installed.

Be very careful and take your time tearing out old cabinets. Electrical wiring is often hidden, plumbing is sometimes routed through cabinets and heating ducts may have been directed under the existing base cabinets.

In the interest of safety, I suggest you turn off the water supply and electrical service to the kitchen area as well as other nearby rooms. This safety measure will help avoid accidents or damage should you inadvertently break a water line or cut a power cable.

Support the upper cabinets with blocks or a strong wooden box prior to removing screws or nails. The sudden weight shift downward when the last fastener is removed can be surprising. Always, if possible, enlist the help of someone to stabilize the cabinet as you remove the fasteners. Also, with respect to upper cabinets, remove all loose assemblies such as shelves so that the cabinet is as light as possible. You'll also avoid the danger of having shelving fall on you should the cabinet suddenly tip. I often remove the cabinet doors prior to removal as well to further lighten the load.

Removing base cabinets can also be hazardous, even though they appear to be sitting on the floor. Rotten floor support systems or poorly connected toe kick platforms may cause the base cabinet to fall forward when the last screw is removed. Again, enlist the aid of another person to support the assembly when removing fastening devices. I've had a cabinet fall because I thought four screws secured the unit when only two were actually anchored into the wall studs. It can be quite a shock and potentially dangerous, so be very careful.

SITE PREPARATION

Site preparation prior to new cabinet installation is a very important process. Verify that water and waste supply lines are in the correct location and electrical service is sufficient and correctly positioned.

If you plan on moving the sink location, now is an excellent time to re-route supply lines. The cabinet system detailed in this book incorporates a full back board on both upper and lower units. Wall sheathing can be removed to allow changes in supply line positioning.

The same is true with electrical service lines. Verify that the outlets are in the correct location and at the correct height. Base cabinet height is 36″, but you must also account for the added height of the countertop backsplash, which can often add an additional 4″ to the overall base height. And if additional electrical service is required, now is an ideal time to have an electrician install new wiring.

Use a long level or straightedge to check the wall condition. You'll never find a perfect wall, but a wall stud that has badly bowed out over time can cause problems during new cabinet installation. If you find a bad bulge in any of the walls, remove the sheeting and correct the problem.

NEW CABINET INSTALLATION

Cabinet installation methods vary, depending on the installer. The primary difference is whether to begin by installing the uppers or the bases. Each method has its merits, as there is no absolute correct way of installing cabinets. Find a process that you are comfortable with to achieve the end result—properly installed cabinets.

I will describe my method of cabinet installation based on our sample kitchen layout. Refer to the side profile drawing of a base and an upper cabinet for basic dimensions.

The Starting Point

There are some considerations that you should be aware of before proceeding. Often a room is out of square and walls are not perfectly plumb. This can cause a number of problems during cabinet installation. Plan on installing cabinets from a point where you won't get boxed in by badly built walls. In our sample kitchen, I would go through the process as described, checking the room dimensions for cabinet runs that are between walls. For example, the N to L base cabinet run is between two walls, so verify that your space requirements are correct as you install each cabinet. It's possible for the wall at L to be out of plumb enough that your cabinet will not fit. It's best to test fit your cabinets prior to anchoring them permanently in place.

In our sample kitchen, the upper cabinet runs are both closed runs. This is typically the most difficult installation. In this situation I would start at cabinet E and work out to both sides, always checking my remaining distances to avoid any serious problems. It can be frustrating if you have to remove installed cabinets to plane a face frame because you've run out of space. This is probably the best reason to accurately measure the room dimensions during your initial planning stage.

1 Determine Level and Plumb

The first step in cabinet installation is to determine the level or slope of the floor and how much the walls are out of plumb. This is your biggest challenge when installing kitchen cabinets. In thirty years of renovation work, I don't believe I've come across a room that had perfectly level floors and plumb walls. Fortunately, the adjustable cabinet legs allow for easier installation as compared to the constructed base support assembly system. And the overhang of the face frame allows room for scribing cabinets to an out-of-plumb wall.

Draw a level line around the room at a reference height of 35¼″ where the base cabinets are to be installed. Measure from the floor to that line at various positions around the room. Determine the highest point in the room. It will be the smallest distance from that level reference line to the floor. All floors have a slope—some are greater than others—and it's important that the high point is determined. If you start installing cabinets in an area other than the high point, you may not have sufficient adjustment range on the cabinet legs.

2 Install the Base Cabinets

Install a base cabinet at the highest point in the room. If you cannot start at the highest point, be aware of the adjustment limits with the cabinet legs. Level that base cabinet and anchor it to the wall.

3 Scribe the Stiles

You may be required to scribe the stile if it isn't tight against the wall, and you might have to use shims between the cabinet back board and the wall to fill gaps. Check the fit after leveling the cabinet and use a compass, adjusted to the widest part of the gap between the

Fig. 17-2

Base cabinets are anchored to the wall studs with 3" screws through the back boards.

Fig. 17-1

Establishing a level line for the base cabinet installation

Fig. 17-3

Scribing a stile to the wall with a compass

wall and stile, as your reference. Holding the point of the compass against the wall, draw a pencil line on the stile face. Use a sharp plane and remove wood up to the pencil line until you get a tight fit. You may find that a belt sander does the job when you have many contours in the wall.

Plane the stile to the line and test fit your cabinet until you achieve a nice tight fit. You can make the fitting process easier by "back planing" the stile edge. That is accomplished by holding the plane or belt sander at a slight angle so that you create a taper from front to back on the stile edge. With this method, you make the front face of the stile the widest part, making wall fitting easier.

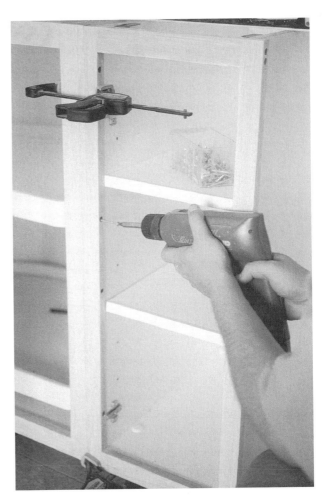

Fig. 17-4

Cabinets are secured to each other through pre-drilled holes with 1¼" wood screws. The countersunk screw hole can be filled with a wood plug if necessary.

4 Join Cabinets Together

Place cabinet M beside cabinet N and adjust the back legs so that the back of the cabinet is even with the cabinet reference line. Adjust the front legs until the cabinet is level, side to side and back to front. Temporarily remove the doors on the cabinets and clamp the left side stile of cabinet N to the right side stile of cabinet M with wooden hand screw clamps.

Drill a ⅛" countersink pilot through one stile and partially into the other. Drill a hole slightly larger than the screw body thickness through the stile on the screw head side to allow the screw to rotate freely in that stile to prevent bridging (the effect caused when the screw threads into both pieces of wood being fastened, preventing the pieces from being drawn tightly together). Fasten the stiles together with three 1¼" screws at the top, middle and bottom. Anchor the cabinet to the wall with 3" screws through the back board and into the wall studs.

5 Complete Base Cabinet Installation

Install the remainder of the base cabinets in the same manner. With respect to the sample layout, set the stile-to-stile spacing between cabinets K and J at 31". This will provide clearance for ⅜" countertop overhang on cabinets K and J and leave a 30¼" space for the stove.

6 Install the Countertop

Install the countertop, scribing and removing material if necessary, so that the countertop fits tightly against the wall. Overhang the small countertop on base cabinet J by ⅜" on each side. Use ⅝" screws in the brackets to secure the countertop in place.

7 Install Upper Cabinets

Mount upper corner cabinet E with four 3" wood screws through the back board into the wall studs. The cabinet must be level and plumb, as it's the reference point for all the upper cabinets. Verify your remaining space after installing each cabinet. Cabinets A and H will probably require stile scribing to get a perfect fit.

Install the remainder of the upper cabinets with the spacer box as an aid. Level the cabinets, screw the adjoining stiles to each other and anchor the cabinets to the wall. The bottoms of the stiles must be even on the cabinets. Reduced-height cabinets (cabinets G, C and A) should be installed so that the top of the cabinets are in line with the other upper cabinets.

8 Install Under-Cabinet Veneer

Install veneer plywood on the underside of all upper cabinets with either contact cement or brad nails. I have also successfully used a high-quality construction cement, which is easier than contact cement and much quicker to apply.

Fig. 17-6
Installing upper cabinets with a shop-made support box

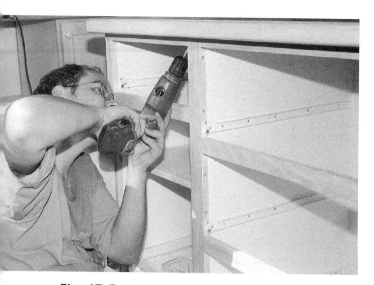

Fig. 17-5
The countertop is secured with ⅝" screws through right-angle brackets.

Fig. 17-7
¼" plywood veneer is applied to the underside of the upper cabinets.

9 Attach Trim Molding

Cut to size and install trim molding on the top edge of the upper cabinets. Any errors in stile length cutting or gaps between the stiles can be left at the top of the cabinets and will be covered by the molding. Trim molding style is dependent on individual taste. I've installed everything from 1″ bead to 4″ crown molding to achieve different finished appearances.

10 Cut Toe Kick Boards

Cut the toe kick boards to length, install the plinth clips and secure the boards to the cabinet legs. Use butt joints where the toe kick boards intersect at right angles. If the floor is out of level, you may have to scribe the bottom of the toe kick board to get a tight fit. You can use quarter-round molding, which is flexible, to fill the gaps between the floor and the toe board. Nail the quarter round to the toe board while holding it tightly against the floor.

11 Install End Cabinet Molding

Install doorstop molding around the perimeter on the exposed base and upper cabinet sides. Use mitered corners with the molding to form a perimeter picture frame. This adds visual depth to the cabinet ends. Any wall irregularities can be hidden, as the molding is slightly flexible and can be pushed into the contours of the wall.

Tip

Build the upper cabinet support box out of 1″ × 6″ softwood slightly smaller than the countertop-to-under-cabinet height. Use cedar shims to raise the upper cabinet into its correct position while it rests on the box. Be careful to support the cabinet during this process. Get someone to assist you at this stage.

It's best to cut and install one molding piece at a time to give you the tightest fit possible.

Fig. 17-8
Install upper trim molding.

Fig. 17-9
Install the toe kick boards using the groove- or screw-on-style leg clips.

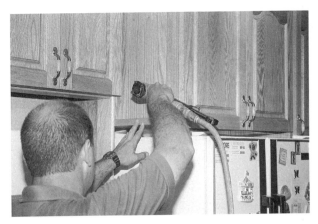

Fig. 17-10
Doorstop molding is applied around the edges of the exposed end cabinet.

12 Install Cabinet Doors

Install the cabinet doors, adjusting for plumb and equal spacing between doors on double-door cabinets. There are normally three adjustment screws on good-quality European hinges. You should be able to adjust the door gap as close as $1/16''$ on two-door cabinets, and that gap must be equal from top to bottom. Humidity variances can cause the door gap to change, which may require occasional adjustments. The climate in your area as well as the control of humidity in your home will have an impact on how much change you'll experience.

13 Install Cabinet Drawers

Install the drawers and check the operation. Drawers can sometimes go out of alignment if the base cabinet was twisted during installation. Proper drawer operation is critical, as this hardware is constantly in use. There's nothing more frustrating than improperly operating cabinet drawers, so buy the best quality drawer slides that you can afford.

14 Check Shelf and Cabinet Alignment

Install the cabinet shelves and verify the alignment. Shelves should rest on all four shelf pins unless they've been thrown out of alignment because the cabinet has been racked or twisted during installation. If severely twisted, the cabinet may have to be loosened from the wall and aligned. Avoid twisting by making sure the cabinet is level and plumb when installed.

It's important that you avoid racking (twisting) the cabinet during installation. Most walls are not straight; many have irregular surfaces and are not plumb. When anchoring cabinets to the wall, verify that the cabinet back is touching the wall; if there is a gap, use a shim to fill the

Fig. 17-11
Replace the doors, checking their fit.

Fig. 17-12
Install the drawers, checking their fit and operation.

space. I find cedar shims work very well because they are tapered. Always check the level, front to back and side to side, as well as the plumb of the cabinet before and after you anchor it securely. Racked cabinets will seriously affect the operation of drawers and the proper position of shelves on the shelf pins. It may also cause doors to be off level, affecting the operation and appearance.

All stiles on adjoining cabinets should be flush on the bottom. If there is an error because stiles were not cut the same length during construction, leave the error at the top of the cabinet. The tops of the stiles on the base cabinets are hidden by the countertop overhang and by the applied trim on the upper cabinets.

There are situations that will arise during cabinet installation, many of which cannot be anticipated. However, you can minimize the "surprises" by taking accurate measurements during the planning stage. Measure wall-to-wall distances at the top, middle and bottom. Use a long level on the floor and against the walls to determine the level and plumb of these surfaces. Review the installation process in your mind before you build the cabinets, checking for electrical wiring needs and problems, sink, water drain and water supply situations. And, most importantly, verify that door openings will allow you to bring cabinets into the kitchen area.

INSTALLING APPLIANCES

Installing appliances is always challenging, particularly when there appears to be a lack of standards with respect to appliance dimensions. In reality, there are a few set standards that manufacturers follow.

Refrigerators

Most refrigerators require 33″ of space for proper installation. Ranges need about 30″, and the majority of dishwashers require a 24″ opening. However, don't assume theses dimensions are cast in stone. Verify your appliance dimensions before beginning the kitchen design process.

Ranges

One common point of frustration in the kitchen cabinetmaking industry is with ranges. Most cabinetmakers will leave 31″ of space between lower cabinets for range placement. This allowance provides for 3/8″ countertop overhang on each cabinet side and 1/4″ clearance between the countertop sides and the range for easy removal and replacement during cleaning. Range hoods are exactly 30″ wide and look properly installed when there isn't any space on either side.

The simplest way I've found to overcome the problem, and to have the upper and lower cabinets line up, is to add 1/2″ to each upper cabinet stile on either side of the over-the-stove cabinet. The upper stove cabinet, being 30″ wide, will allow installation of the range hood without space on each side. The added stile width (now a 1 1/2″ stile) on each of the upper cabinets to the right and left of the upper stove cabinet will force them in line with the lower cabinets. This added stile width is only on the upper cabinet's side that butts against the upper stove cabinet.

Countertop ranges, built-in wall ovens and microwaves don't seem to follow any set dimensional standards. It's best to refer to the installation instructions when designing your kitchen so that you are aware of the requirements.

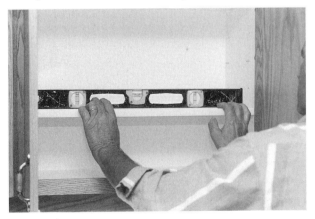

Fig. 17-13
Verify that cabinets have remained level and plumb during the installation.

LIST OF SUPPLIERS

Following is a list of suppliers for the various materials used in building these cabinets. In some cases the manufacturers of the products are listed. These manufacturers do not necessarily sell their goods directly to woodworkers, but have dealer networks. Contact the company for information on their method of sales and request the name of their distributor in your area.

Adams & Kennedy Co. Ltd.
6178 Regional Rd. 8, Box 700
Manotick, Ontario K4M 1A6
Canada
(613) 822-6800
Particle core board, hardwood, molding, cabinet doors

Amerock Co.
4000 Auburn St.
Rockford, IL 61125
(815) 969-6212
Lazy susans, cabinet storage accessories, door handles, hardware

Blum Canada Inc.
7135 Pacific Circle,
Mississauga, Ontario L5T 2A8
Canada
(416) 670-7920
Drawer glides, adjustable legs, hinges

Julius Blum Inc.
Hwy. 16 Lowesville
Stanley, NC 28164
(800) 438-6788
Hinges, drawer slides and all other cabinetmaking hardware

Canadian Kitchen Cabinet Assoc.
27 Goulburn Ave.
Ottawa, Ontario K1N 8C7
Canada
(613) 233-6205
Trade association

Caron Industries
45, 4E Rue
Montmagny, Quebec G5V 3S3
Canada
(800) 463-7060
Cabinet doors

Cefaloni Countertops
Unit 1 - 174 Colonade Road
Ottawa, Ontario K2E 7J5
Canada
(613) 727-5234
Countertops, laminates and solid-surface countertops

Custom Service Hardware
1214 Hwy. 143
Cedarburg, WI 53012
(414) 375-7960
Kitchen cabinetmaking hardware

Dayvan Inc.
33 Dufflaw Rd.,
Toronto, Ontario M6A 2W2
Canada
(416) 781-9118
Kitchen cabinetmaking hardware

Dimar Canada Ltd.
260 Spinnaker Way, Unit 9
Concord, Ontario L4K 4M1
Canada
(416) 738-7919
Carbide drill bits, saw blades, router bits

Elias Woodwork
Box 1659
Winkler, Manitoba R6W 4B5
Canada
(800) 665-0623
Cabinet doors

Fitzpatrick & Weller Inc.
12 Mill St., P.O. Box 490
Ellicottville, NY 14731
(716) 699-2393
Cabinet doors

Grass Canada Inc.
7270 Tobram Rd., Unit 17
Mississauga, Ontario L4T 3Y7
Canada
(800) 387-3408
Hinges, drawer glides

Hafele America
3901 Cheyenne Dr.
Archdale, NC 27263
(800) 334-1873
Hinges, drawer glides, screws

Hafele Canada Inc.
6345 Netherhart Rd.
Mississauga, Ontario L5T 1B8
Canada
(416) 564-9830
Hinges, drawer glides, screws

Hardware International
123 E. First St.
North Vancouver, British Columbia V7L 1B2
Canada
(604) 654-5100
Kitchen cabinetmaking hardware

Kenlin Enterprises Inc.
1530 Old Skokie Rd.
Highland Park, IL 60035
(708) 831-2300
Base levelers, drawer glides, hinges

Lee Valley Tools Ltd.
Ottawa, Toronto, London, Calgary, Edmonton,
Vancouver
Canada
(800) 267-8761
Kitchen cabinetmaking hardware, tools and
equipment

Liberty Hardware Mfg. Corp.
923 Alton Place
High Point, NC 27263
(919) 434-5051
Kitchen cabinetmaking hardware

Martin Hardware Distributors Ltd.
5915 Wallace St.
Mississauga, Ontario L4Z 1Z8
Canada
(416) 890-4920
Complete line of cabinetmaking hardware, including screws

Rev-a-Shelf Inc.
P.O. Box 99585
Jefferson, KY 40269
(800) 626-1126
Excellent quality lazy susan and flip-out
assemblies

Richelieu Hardware Ltd.
1910 Hymus Blvd.
Dorval, Quebec H9A 1X6
Canada
(514) 683-4144
Complete line of cabinetmaking hardware, including screws

White Oak Custom Woodworking
160 Doughton Rd.
Concord, Ontario L4K 1R3
Canada
(800) 205-DOOR
Cabinet doors

Wood Technology Inc.
P.O. Box 1301, Elf Way
Pittsboro, NC 27312
(800) 231-9522
Appliance lifts, drawer linings, knobs and pulls,
adjustable legs

Woodworker's Hardware
P.O. Box 784
St. Cloud, MN 56302
(800) 383-0130
Mail order, complete line of hardware and
accessories

The Woodworkers' Store
21801 Industrial Blvd.
Rogers, MN 55374
(800) 279-4441
Hardware and supplies

Woodworker's Supply
5604 Alameda Place, NE
Albuquerque, NM 87113
(800) 645-9292
Hardware and supplies

THE INFORMATION HIGHWAY

If you have questions or comments concerning this publication, or you just need a little help with a special situation, you can contact the author via the Internet.

Danny Proulx can be reached at his E-mail address, **danny@cabinetmaking.com**. You can also visit his home page through the Web at **http://www.cabinetmaking.com**.

Comments concerning your project are always appreciated, and Danny will be glad to offer some free advice if needed.

INDEX

More Great Books for Your Woodshop!